SECURITY AND LAW ENFORCEMENT

About the Author

Sankar Sen is a distinguished member of the Indian Police Service. He was the Director of National Police Academy, Hyderabad and Director General of the National Human Rights Commission. He was awarded the Police Medal for Meritorious Services and President's Medal for Distinguished Service. He has authored a number of books. Shri Sen was deeply involved in the human rights sensitisation programmes for police and para-military forces and improvement of prison administration. A large number of his articles on police reforms, law enforcement and human rights have appeared in national dailies and magazines in India and abroad. Some of his publications include, *Indian Police Today, Police in a Democratic Society, Trafficking in Women and Children* and *Enforcing Police Accountability through Civilian Oversight.*

SECURITY AND LAW ENFORCEMENT

Sankar Sen

CONCEPT PUBLISHING COMPANY PVT. LTD.
NEW DELHI - 110 059

ISBN: 978-93-6344-056-2

First Published 2026

Published and Printed by

Concept Since1974

Concept Publishing Company Pvt. Ltd.
A/15-16, Commercial Block, Mohan Garden
New Delhi-110059 (India)
T: +91-11-41101460
E: publishing@conceptpub.com, *W*: www.conceptpub.com

Cataloging in Publication--Courtesy: D.K. Agencies (P) Ltd. <docinfo@dkagencies.com>

Sen, Sankar, 1936- **author.**
Security and law enforcement / Sankar Sen.
pages cm
Includes index.
ISBN 9789363440562

1. Law enforcement--India--Uttar Pradesh. 2. Law enforcement--India. 3. Human rights--India--Uttar Pradesh. 4. Human rights--India. I. Title.

LCC HV8249.U88S43 2026 | DDC 363.209542 23

Preface

The book is a collection of articles published in national dailies on various issues concerning law enforcement, policing, corruption and moments of triumph and tragedy in the lives of police officers.

In the first two decades of the 21st century, policing in India, has become increasingly tough, complex and challenging. There is serious escalation of crime and violence. The police and the security forces are locked in a grim battle with the *Jihadi* terrorists and the Maoists and other subversive elements.

There are also many other chinks in the national internal security architecture. Neglect of police reforms is making the police dysfunctional and politicized and not able to cope with growing internal threats and challenges. I do hope that the articles in the book will be of interest to security and law enforcement officers, academics as well as informed members of the public, and stimulate reflection over the issues concerning national security.

The capacity of the police to intervene promptly and effectively in public agitation, communal riots and other difficult law and order situations is undermined by constant political interference in its statutory functioning. The police in the country now function as the agents of the political party in power and not people's police. This has alienated the police from the public and crippled its effectiveness. And this is in sharp contrast with the working of the police in advanced democratic countries, where operational independence of the police is considered sacrosanct.

Policing in the country, in the 21st century, has to develop in many ways and directions, and without meaningful police reforms, the governance of the country will not improve. It is hoped that the thoughts and views contained in these articles will encourage further thinking on these issues by the law enforcement officers and policy-makers and help in evolving more appropriate strategies to deal with them.

Sankar Sen

Contents

Section 2

Section 3

Section 1

1

Misdirected War against Criminals in U.P.

The police in Uttar Pradesh have launched a vigorous crackdown on criminals after the Chief Minister of U.P. Yogi Adityanath has declared to make the state free of crime and criminals. Inspired by the edict of the Chief Minister, the police chief of the state has directed his officers and men to go hammer and tongs after the criminals. The upshot is that some criminals have been killed in encounters and many, out of fear of being gunned down, have surrendered. According to date, sourced from Police Headquarters, as many as 1,142 encounters were recorded between March 2017 and January this year, and 38 alleged criminals were killed. Eight were killed in the last five days. Encounter specialists in the police are calling the shots. Encounters took place in Lucknow, Saharanpur, Gorakhpur, Baghpat and other areas of the state. Many criminals, out of fear, are surrendering, and many have given undertaking to the police that they would not indulge in crimes, any further.

Though the Chief Minister has given a green signal and assured support to the police, these developments are worrying and should not make one oblivious of the hard fact that police encounters are counter-productive and have many deleterious consequences. It is true that there is tacit public approval behind police encounters. Members of the public welcome the encounters as they feel that criminals must get their just deserts. The wheels of criminal justice move at a snail's pace. Trials drag on interminably. Notorious criminals get away scot-free and cock a snook at the justice delivery system. The fact of the matter is that encounters are not the problem, but symptoms of the collapsing system of justice and public demand for quick solutions to the law and order problems.

For proper and efficient functioning of the police, illegal encounters have to be firmly discouraged and not encouraged by the police leaders and professionals. They generate lawlessness within the police and breed contempt for law. To break law in the name of law enforcement has no place in a democratic society governed by the rule of law. It is objectionable because it is arbitrary as a process, and random in its effects. It is aptly said that a democratic order maintained by repression and criminality is ultimate disorder because it creates a link between social order and atrocities. The National Police Commission, in its report (Fifth Report), has perceptively observed that fake encounters have to be discouraged by the police leaders as this is not the remedy for the situation. Answer is to strengthen law and the legal process.

There is a wrong public perception that all police encounters are fake and stage-managed. There are genuine encounters when the police and security personnel attacked by the criminals exercise their right of private defence. Such encounters are justified within the framework of law with reference to Sections 97, 100 and 103 of IPC, which deal with the right of private defence of life and property. Section 46(3) of CRPC empowers police to use force to the extent of causing death to a person accused of an offence punishable with death or imprisonment for life, if such a person evades arrest, or seeks to escape arrest. Thus, legal provision exists for use of force against the terrorists and criminals that may result in their death. Thus encounters, *per se,* are not illegal.

The National Human Rights Commission, on receiving complaints of false police encounters from Andhra Pradesh Civil Liberties Committee (APCLC), regarding false encounters staged by Andhra police, it held public hearings in Hyderabad and recorded evidence. The Chairman of NHRC, in a letter to the Chief Ministers, advised them to issue directions to all the police stations on the procedures that should be followed with regard to cases where death had been caused in encounters with the police. The Commission felt that the right of private defence should not be manipulated to justify fake encounters, and the procedures of Section 46(3) of the Criminal Procedure Code should not be subverted to such an end. The procedure outlined by NHRC lays down that in the case of an encounter in which the police are involved, immediate steps should be taken to investigate the facts and circumstances leading to death, and ascertain how the offence was committed and by whom. If police officers belonging to the same police station are members of the encounter party, it will be appropriate that other police agencies, preferably the state CID, should take over investigation of such cases. Unfortunately, these salutary instructions of the NHRC remain just paper instruction, and are honoured in breach. It is not known if NHRC has taken any firm and tangible measures to ensure that its mandatory instructions are acted upon. The upshot is that tough counter-measures involving brazen violation of human rights are advocated by the police leaders and their political bosses against the criminals on the dubious ground that the latter have scant respect for human rights.

The practice of violating law, in the name of better law enforcement, is a mistaken strategy, fraught with perilous consequences. It will be arbitrary and random and will have the effect of undermining police professionalism and efficiency and encouraging lawlessness in the force. In my long years of service in the police and an innings in the NHRC, I have witnessed that, police vested with the unbridled authority to use force, become trigger-happy, and run berserk. In the name of combating crime and criminals, the police have settled old scores. Many innocent people have suffered loss of lives and limbs. Again, research study by a former DGP of Maharashtra police has unveiled how in

Mumbai the police joined hands with one group of the underworld to eliminate their rivals in fake encounters.

There is another downside. Violating the rule of law will have the effect of making police scapegoats. Police officers rightly complain of inadequacies of law, and handcuffing of police by law. But they forget that when police take resort to extra-legal tactics to make up the deficiencies of law and legal procedures, they are trying to remedy the inadequacies they did not create. By resorting to illegal methods and exceeding their mandate, they not only take responsibility for crime on themselves but deflect attention to themselves for omissions of others. Again, serious violation of law, when discovered, invites outside interventions and the police officers, in trying to fend off such interventions, develop a "bunker mentality" and become less willing to be transparent. Putting it aptly, the American scholar, David Bayley, has said that "Illegality in the service of public safety makes policing a furtive and anxious activity and undermines pride which is the basis of job satisfaction."

It is reported that some retired senior police officers of U.P. have warned the police force of the risks and dangers inherent in the abuse and misuse of power. Some trigger-happy officers are likely to come to grief in due course for their overzealousness. At that time, the political masters will not come to their rescue. They will rue like Cardinal Wolsey for their unthinking loyalty to the King, and not to the canons of law!

2

Police Autonomy and Accountability in a Democracy

Sacking of the former British Home Secretary Suella Braverman by the Prime Minister Rishi Sunak brings into focus the issue of police autonomy and accountability in a democratic government. Her dismissal came after Braverman wrote an Opinion piece in the *Times* of London in which she blamed the Metropolitan police for "playing favourites" to the Palestinian Protesters whom she described as "hate marchers". The Minister's action invited strong criticisms from MPs cutting across party line.

The pro-Palestine protesters were gathering in London every weekend to demand a halt to Israel's air and ground offensive against Hamas ruled Gaza. The Sunak government viewed the programme as disruptive and wanted the police to ban it. But the London police Chief Mark Rowley categorically maintained that any ban would require intelligence "threat of serious disorder and so far that threshold has not been crossed". The Government did not try to override the police decision. The Prime Minister said that Britain must "remain true to the right to protest and free speech even if we do not agree with them."

The role of the police in a democratic society is difficult, complex and can be unbelievably thankless. From no other profession so much is demanded with so little recompense. The police have to work in an ever-changing society. To quote the Royal Commission on Police "There is nothing constant about the range and variety of police duties just as there is nothing constant about the patterns and hidden trends in society that dispose man to crime." Further, policing today requires a high degree of professionalism. The old concept of police man as a "Renaissance Man" who once he affixes his badge has become magically able to perform any job has to be done away with. Police officers also enjoy awesome authority in matters relating to life and liberty of the citizens. Hence, it is essential that police should act within the four corners of law and respect the constitutional rights of the citizens. In a democratic state there should not be any interference from anywhere in discharge of the lawful functions of the police. Totalitarian states are called police states because the police enjoy not only unbridled authority but remain vulnerable to extralegal pressures and influence.

In Great Britain, the Royal Commission of Police (1962) in its Final Report stated "The case of *Fisher* v. *Oldham Corporation* established that whatever else he might be, the constable was not a servant of any organ of the government.

Not only in the United Kingdom but in other democratic countries like Canada, New Zealand etc., the police forces are independent operationally and only respond to operational directives emanating from within the force. In Japan, police authorities themselves are virtually sovereign in respect of internal control. Though there are Public Safety Commissions to oversee overall management of the force, the police authorities are supreme in respect of internal control.

In Indian democracy, however, the situation remains different and dismal ... Constant interference in police work by the political masters has made police ineffective and has totally eroded its autonomy. Section 3 of the Police Act of 1861 provides that the superintendence of police shall vest in and be exercised by the State Government. This provision of the Act has been unabashedly used to interfere in the regular working of the police. In the words of a perceptive American police scholar David Bayley, "The rule of law in modern India has been undermined by the rule of politics", instead of rapidly transforming the Organisation of the Police after independence, the same system which the British had created in 1861, continues. The control mechanism of the British Raj was invigorated by the new political dispensation. It is interesting to note that the Chief Minister of almost every state has taken charge of the police..This is a dramatic indication of the importance of police in Political life in contemporary India.

The National Police Commission made some pertinent and significant recommendations to insulate the police from extraneous pressures and influence and to ensure its independence in the operational areas of police investigation. The National Human Rights Commission also endorsed these crucial recommendations. The Supreme Court in the case of *Prakash Singh and others* vs. *Union of India* issued some clear directives to State governments to implement these recommendations and laid down mechanisms to insulate the police from extraneous pressures, but the political masters have through various devices tried to stall and scuttle them. Some states have enacted new police Acts which are more retrogressive than the Police Act of 1861. They want the *status quo* to continue and keep their firm stranglehold over the police. They tend to forget that the ruling party's police can never command support and confidence of the people.

But along with police autonomy there must be police accountability, as the National Police Commission has mentioned in its report, means answerability for the proper performance of the assigned task. While it is true that the ultimate responsibility of the police is to the people, the police have the proximate responsibility to the law of the land which is the expression of the popular will. It is aptly said that the relationship of the police to law is instrumental as well as professional. It is a tool in their hands for initiating action against the offending members of the public while it also lays down the standards under which police will exercise their functions.

Indeed an independent and abusive police poses a fundamental problem for the legitimacy of the legal and political order.

The fact International Human Rights Standards also firmly emphasise police accountability. Universal Declaration of Human Rights, Convention on Torture, Code of Conduct for Law Enforcement Officers, condemn abuse of authority or use of unnecessary and excessive force by the police. In India, the Code for Law Enforcement Officials has been incorporated in the Code of Conduct for Police Officials issued by the Ministry of Home Affairs.

For ensuring police accountability people have to be made aware of their rights and they should be willing to exercise the same in a responsible manner. Public awareness also must involve realisation of the problems and constraints under which the police function. The police in their turn must also try to understand as observed by the National Police Commission, "their ultimate accountability is to the people and people alone. Their accountability to law and to the organisation is only complementary to the ultimate objective of accountability to the people."

3

Police Reforms

A Categorical Imperative

Directives of the Supreme Court on Police Reforms, recommended by the National Police Commission have been perfunctorily implemented in most of the states. The Apex Court had issued clear directives to the Central and State governments to insulate the police from extraneous pressures and influence, by implementing the core reforms recommended by the National Police Commission (1978-1981). Important directives of the court in Prakash Singh's case, included, *inter alia*, fixed tenure of two years for DG of Police, separation of law and order from the investigation wing of the police, setting up Police Establishment Boards to decide transfers, postings and other service-related matters of police officers up to the rank of Deputy Superintendent of the Police and appointment of State Security Commissions to ensure that the political executives are not able to exert unwarranted, baneful pressure and influence on police. Unfortunately, recommendations of the Apex Court remained unimplemented. Most of the state governments dragged their feet, and tried to scuttle reforms under various pretexts. The truth of the matter is that political masters did not want to give up their stranglehold over the police. The Apex Court also failed to crack the whip and force the recalcitrant states to implement the directives of the Court. It refrained from adopting a tough, no-nonsense line and extended time-lines for implementation of reforms by the state governments. Very recently, the Court has again intervened and directed that the state governments shall not arbitrarily appoint heads of police forces and laid down a set of guidelines that made it necessary for the state governments to get a nod of the Union Police Service Commission before filling up the post of the top cop. However, in view of the determined opposition of the political masters, it would be very difficult to implement core structural reforms in the police only on the strength of the directives of the court. The road ahead is going to be bumpy and the outcome uncertain. But the issue of police reforms has to be viewed in a wider perspective. The ambit of police reforms need not be confined only to insulation of the police from extraneous political pressures, though this is an imperative reform. There are many other areas of policing crying for reforms, where determined police leaders can usher in reforms and qualitatively improve the functioning of the police.

An essential police reform that brooks no delay in empowerment of the police constabulary. Police constables constitute almost 70 per cent of the police force. The constables of the present day have moved far from the predominantly mechanical roles assigned to them in 1902 Police Commission. They now interact with the people in a variety of situations where they have to apply their mind and exercise judgement and enforce law with public understanding and cooperation. Any reform and restructuring of the police system will not last unless the mass base of the pyramid is rendered healthy and efficient.

It is a sad fact that a large number of constables retire in the same rank after more than thirty years of service. They may not get promotion even by one rank in their entire service career. Thus, this promotional structure in the police system does not enable and fulfil their legitimate career ambitions. The police constable must cease, as David Bayley has said, to remain as "spear carriers in the police drama. They have to be major actors standing at the centre of the stage."

The Second Administrative Reforms Commission, in its report on public order, has strongly advocated the need to upgrade the skill and training of the constables. It recommended that instead of recruiting constables, who are matriculates, it would be better to recruit graduates at the starting point of the civil police, and give them the stature, assistance and respect. It calculated that about 700 graduate Assistant Sub Inspectors can be recruited against vacancies of 1,000 Constables, without any serious financial burden. There are other in-house reforms that can be implemented, without any serious impediment.

There is also acute shortage of manpower. A large number of vacancies exist in different ranks. In India, ratio of ordinary policemen for 1,000 people is 1.2, i.e. little about half the level, recommended by the UN. Most of the officers and men are overworked and underpaid. They get no overtime allowance for extra hours put in by them. There are research studies showing that recent introduction of 8-hour shift in the State of Kerala, and in the city of Mumbai, has radically improved performance.

Police training is another area where reforms are overdue. Most of the state police training institutions are in a poor shape and ill-managed. "Police training has remained", as described in the report of the Gore Committee, "a ritual where unwilling and ill-equipped instructors are performing the rites of training and drilling to unwilling trainees." Further, most of the state institutions have become dumping grounds for inefficient and corrupt officers who transmit negative values to the trainees. In order to play the role of change agents, the trainers have to be picked up carefully. Gore Committee recommended suitable incentives including rent-free accommodation, special pay and recognition in the form of subsequent promotion and good posting for the trainers with a view to inducting the best available talents. Unfortunately, except in some central training institutions, incentives are not given in a regular way to the trainers. Very often, officers view posting in training institutions as punishment.

Though training is an important input for improving and optimising work performance of officers and men, it can, however, be effective, only when the organization has faith in it, and there is an organizational climate that encourages observance of principles taught during training. Unfortunately, over the years, an organizational climate and culture has grown up in the police, that does on frown upon abuse and misuse of force. Human rights culture in the police is poor, if not non-existent. A heavy responsibility rests upon senior officers to build a congenial organizational climate. Even now, in police forces of the country, policemen are appreciated for "hard-nosed policing". In many police organizations, rough and ready use of force, meet with peer approval. In order to gain peer approval, officers become over-assertive, and dispensers of rough and ready street justice, which alienates the police from the public. Police scholars, like Niederhoffer, have felt that many police officers, who constantly witness man's inhumanity to man, become disoriented, and display violent tricks in their encounter with citizens. It is this unnecessary and avoidable use of force that causes considerable friction between the police and the community. This is an area where an urgent change in police culture is called for. Research on the use of deadly force has shown that strict administrative control has a restraining effect on the frequency with which officers use firearms.

In Indian police, peer group supervision is conspicuously missing. Peer supervision can be a powerful tool in ensuring police accountability and all-around good policing. In Japan, police officers work in pairs, with the understanding that one officer is responsible for ensuring the correct work and conduct of the other. In India also, policemen work in groups, but the ethos is against the assumption of mutual responsibility.

Another urgent reform is an all-out crusade against police corruption. Police corruption—corruption in the police is not a new phenomenon. Even the Police Commission in 1902 spoke about alarming corruption and malpractices of the police Darogas. The Bihar Police Commission (1960) quoted the saying of Sir John

Shore, "The subordinate police officers in India were paid so low, as almost to justify corruption." Even in the early sixties, when I had joined service and posted in Orissa, the number of officers of questionable integrity could be counted on fingers. The situation during the last two decades has dramatically changed. A nexus has developed between the political masters and police officers of different ranks. The problem is compounded by the fact that many senior police officers are now indulging in brazen acts of corruption by joining hands with the subordinate officers. This is ominous because corruption has a systemic character to it. Once it gets started, it tends to spread in the organization, affecting all its parts. Further, it has a pre-emptive quality. It prevents police leaders from exercising effective control over their subordinates, and curtail the organization's capacity of dealing with various problems afflicting it. Unfortunately, senior officers of questionable integrity are favoured by politicians as they prove to be more malleable and amenable to pressures.

Another reform is for the supervisory officers to vigorously decry 'noble cause corruption'. Noble corruption in policing is defined as corruption committed in the name of good ends; corruption that happens in order to get the bad guys of the street. Noble cause corruption implies faith in the concept that the end justifies the means. The fact is often forgotten that adoption of impermissible means may ultimately undermine the end.

Some justify torture to fight terrorism, and have argued that torture is justified in rare cases where there is "ticking bomb urgency". But the hard fact is that once a degree of torture is permitted, it gives licence to the interrogator to use it systematically and abusively. It is seen that corruption, and particularly noble cause corruption, occurs in an atmosphere of arrogance, which generates a belief that police officers know what is best for society, and have the power and influence to punish anyone, who, according to their perception, constitute a threat to public order and safety. This is an area where senior officers have to take a resolute stand against misconduct and illegal practices of the subordinates.

Over the years also, there has been steady decline in police professionalism. This is an area which requires sustained attention of the police leaders. Police can command awe and respect only when it is professionally competent, and can measure up to the challenges posed by criminals and law-breakers. Common people in a democratic society form their impression of the government by the manner in which the police function, as to most of the people police represent their most dramatic contact with the government. "To consider police as sub-professional, which is commonly the case down the world, is a mistake. It ensures that responsibility of the police will not be discharged with proper creativity and sensitivity."

Another much-needed reform is to make police accountable. In a democratic government, as has been perceptively stated in the report of the Independent Commission for Policing in Northern Ireland, 1994 (Patten Report), police should be accountable in two senses—the subordinate, or obedient sense, and the explanatory, or cooperative sense. In the subordinate sense, the police are employed by the community to provide the service and the community should have means to ensure that it gets service it needs. The police are also subordinate to law just as ordinary citizens are. There should be robust arrangements to ensure effective policing because policing is not a task for police alone. Indeed accountability does not weaken but strengthen the police. Repressive police forces are weak police forces, through they operate under the illusion of strength. Civilians' fear represents the source of weakness. People, who fear the police, do not cooperate with the police in their investigation. Strong police forces function successfully because of the help and cooperation of the citizens they serve.

The National Human Rights Commission recommended establishment of District Complaints Authorities to ensure speedy enquiry into complaints against the police and speedy relief to the victims. Similar directives had been issued by the Supreme Court in the case of Prakash Singh. But both the State Governments and police leadership are unwilling to establish such mechanisms on the specious plea that this will go to demoralize the police. They forget that an accountable police will command greater respect and cooperation from the public than an unfriendly and unaccountable police. Totalitarian states are called police states because the police remain beholden to certain individuals and groups and remain vulnerable to pressures from them.

Indeed, police reforms is a categorical imperative. Without meaningful police reforms good governance of the country would remain a utopia. Many reforms can be brought about by police leaders. In the police, there are many committed police officers and men, who are keen to bring about changes. Apathy of the civil society to the problems and constraints of the police is disheartening. However, only pressures and efforts from within can bring about some important reforms in the police. But at the same time, the exertions for insulation of the police from political pressures and influence must continue uninterruptedly.

The Supreme Court, off and on, has intervened in the sphere of police reforms. It took up as early as in for hearing the petition of Shri Prakash Singh, a retired Director General of Police, urging early implementation of some of the core recommendations of the National Police Commission by the Central and State governments. The court took a long time to make up its mind, and after a prolonged gap of nearly ten years, it issued directives to the Centre and State governments to insulate the police from extraneous pressures and influence by implementing core reforms recommended by the National Police Commission (1978-1981) to insulate the police from extraneous pressures and influence. The Apex Court felt that non-implementation of the core recommendations of the NPC was having an adverse impact on the law enforcement and order maintenance in the country. The important directives of the Apex Court included, *inter alia*, fixed tenure of two years for Director General of Police, unless promoted or removed on disciplinary grounds, separation of the law and order from the investigation wing of the police, setting up of Police Establishment Board to decide transfer, posting and other service-related matters of police officers up to the rank of Deputy Superintendents of Police, and establishment of State Security Commissions to preclude the political, executives to exert unwarranted pressure and influence on police work and administration.

The Court felt that without these structural reforms recommended by the NPC, the police will not be able to function objectively and only serve as hand-maids of the politicians in power. Indeed, this is the sad reality of the police working in the country. Today, it functions as the ruling party's police and not champions of the rights of the people guaranteed by the Constitution. It is viewed as a bogey man—a long arm of the state, to quote the words of 1902 Police Commission, as a long arm of the state that harasses and not befriends the people.

It was hoped that the directives of the Apex Court will usher in a new dawn for Indian Police. It will regain and refurbish its image and be able to function as a neutral and apolitical force committed to fair and non-partisan law enforcement. But this hope was belied. Most of the state governments dragged their feet and tried to scuttle reforms under various pretexts. They did not want to give up their stranglehold over the police. They averred that they support the spirit of reforms but object to some of the directives of the Court. States like Gujarat, Karnataka, Uttar Pradesh, Nagaland questioned the *raison d'etre* of State Security Commissions and some brazenly stated that no unwarranted influence is at all exercised over the police. Many of the states enacted new Police Acts which ran contrary to the spirit of the directives of the Apex Court. In short, most of the state governments wanted to scuttle the proposed reforms instead of implementing them. Police Complaints Authorities have not been set up, as directed by the Apex Court, in most of the states that have enacted laws.

The Supreme Court, urged by the petitioners, set up a monitoring Committee under K.T. Thomas, a former Supreme Court Judge, to monitor the implementation of the Court's directives. The Monitoring Committee found to its dismay that no state has fully implemented the directives of the court and tried to either dilute or side step them. The Committee checked up the ground realities in respect of implementation in four states, viz. Uttar Pradesh, Maharashtra, Karnataka and West Bengal, found that the level of compliance was just marginal and there was total indifference exhibited by the states with regard to police reforms. The Apex Court, however, refrained from adopting a tough no-nonsense line, and extended time frames for implementation of the reforms by the recalcitrant state governments.

Very recently, the Apex Court has again intervened and issued further directive that the state governments shall not arbitrarily appoint heads of police forces and laid down a set of guidelines that would make it necessary for the state governments to get the nod of the Union Public Service Commission before filling up the post of the top cops. State governments will have to prepare a list of three suitable officers three months before the retirement of the incumbent DGP and obtain the approval of the UPSC and then appoint one of the officers from the list as the police chief. The court frowned on the present practice followed by many states to appoint an acting DGP pending the formal appointment and later make him permanent before his superannuation. This enables the state Chief Minister to have a puppet DGP dancing to his tune.

The path of police reforms is going to be bumpy and tortuous. For more than a decade, the Centre and State governments have stalled police reforms and evaded implementation of the Apex Court's directives and various pleas and pretexts. The same stalling tactics and insidious efforts to scuttle the reforms will continue because the political bosses feel that without a subservient police at their beck and call they will be rendered effete and impotent. The Supreme Court so far has not adopted a tough line towards the errant states and is unlikely to do so in future. It does not want a confrontation with the state chief ministers and fears to open a Pandora's box. For the success of police reforms, people's support is imperative and so far this is not forthcoming. The public fear of abusive police authority untrammelled by political control has to be exorcised. For realising this goal there is crying need for police-public relationship at the cutting edge level. Police have to be fair, compassionate and sensitive towards the members of the public particularly the cowering marginalised groups. People's demand for emancipating the police from the vice grip of the politicians will impart a new momentum to the cause of police reforms.

Again mere rules and directives to insulate police from political control will not work unless the police leaders stand up to pressures and oppose unlawful interference in their professional work and refuse to carry out brazenly illegal orders. At present, senior police officers are crawling when they are asked to bend. I know of cases where the State Governments have set up Police Establishment Board headed by a very senior police officer as directed by the Apex Court but the Board has abdicated its mandate and faithfully carries out transfers and postings of subordinate ranks as desired by the Chief Minister. With such weak-kneed leaders at the top mere judicial directives will not bring about the desired change. It is necessary for the police chiefs to have a healthy equation with the political boss for smooth and efficient functioning of the force without being subservient. Some outstanding police chiefs like K.F. Rustamji, B.N. Mullick, D.P. Kohli, N. Saksena wear close to the politicians but have rendered yeoman service to the police. Their contribution remains unforgotten.

4

Death in Police Custody

Why Police do not Change?

Recently, in a case, the CBI Court in Kerala sentenced to death two police officers for custodial killing a person. In this case, a scrap dealer earlier arrested by the police had to be released as he was found innocent, but he had to pay the price through his life when he demanded return of money extorted from him by the police. He was taken to Fort Police Station in Thiruvananthapuram and brutally tortured him to death. The brave mother of the victim courageously and doggedly pursued the case which, after 13 years, ended in the death sentence of the accused persons. This is not perhaps the first case where death sentence has been awarded to serving police officers for brutal crimes committed by them. I recollect a case investigated by the National Human Rights Commission's investigation staff, and subsequently by Bihar State's CID, in which a notorious police sub-inspector was awarded death sentence by the lower court for gunning down a businessman, who refused to pay the extortion money, but death sentence was subsequently commuted to life imprisonment by the higher court.

Deaths in police custody in the country continue unabated and merit a searching analysis of the reasons behind it. Is it just police perversity or outcome of systemic malaise? The National

Human Rights Commission had issued directions as early as in 1993, directing all state governments that any death in police or jail custody should be reported to the Commission within 24 hours. The Collectors and Superintendents of Police were clearly warned that failure on their part to report any custodial death would force the Commission to draw an adverse presumption. NHRC's records show that a total of 2,860 deaths in police custody had been reported by various state governments during the period between March 1993 and 2013. It gives an annual average of about 147 deaths in police custody. This has been, by and large, the pattern in subsequent years also. It is true that all cases of deaths in police custody are not the outcome of only custodial violence by the police. Some arrestees commit suicide or die due to ailments from which they were already suffering. Many such cases reported by the state authorities are closed by the NHRC without ordering any monetary compensation. But the stark fact remains that torture causes many deaths in police custody. Despite punishment of some errant police officers by the courts, firm directives of the Apex Court, slew of recommendations of National and State Human Rights Commissions, issuance of copious police orders and circulars, the scenario remains unchanged. Custodial deaths due to police violence continue to occur in different parts of the country and mire police with eternal shame and infamy. Severely berating custodial torture, the Supreme Court had aptly said, "Nothing is more cowardly and unconscionable than a person in police custody being beaten up, and nothing inflicts a deeper wound on our constitutional culture than a state official running berserk regardless of human rights" (*Kishore Singh* vs. the *State of Rajasthan*). Though instances of custodial torture and violence by the police are now coming to notice with increasing frequency, it will be worthwhile to remember that the evil is not of recent origin. It was, though not widely publicised, very much prevalent in the past. The Torture Commission (1850) highlighted wide prevalence of torture in the police stations of Madras Presidency, and the Indian Police Commission (1902-03) also expressed serious concern about prevalence of torture and deaths in Police stations. Reports of custodial torture by the police received from various parts of the country purvey the unfortunate impression that the police forces in our country are full of sadists and maniacs, who relish the sight of broken skulls. This notion, however, is misleading. Just as there are some violence-prone bad apples, there are also a large number of upright police men who perform their arduous and thankless job respecting human rights. But pressures on the police mount whenever there is a surge in crime and lawlessness. There is public outcry against the police for its ineptitude and a demand that the police will deliver the result by apprehending the alleged criminals and bringing them to book, if necessary, by adopting extra-legal methods. Political masters also press hard on the police to ensure that criminals get their just deserts, and wink at the lawlessness of the police. A perceptive writer on Police psychology (Ben Whiteakerhas) aptly observed that "Janus-like, we have always turned two faces towards a police man." Because of incompatible demands of the public, some policemen become stoically immune to criticisms. There is also an undercurrent of feeling among the police officers that it will be very difficult to prove and nail them for the atrocities committed within the confines of police stations. Other police colleagues including the seniors will rally round them and try to whitewash their omissions and commissions. The "blue code of silence" will rule. Very few members of the public will muster courage to depose against them. This explains as to why in very few cases charges of custodial deaths and torture against the police are proved and they are visited with punishment. The National Police Commission analysed complaints of police torture and custodial deaths in eight states, and found that the charges against the aberrant police personnel could not be proved in most of the cases. Only in some judicial enquiries, they were found guilty, but seldom in departmental enquiries, which drag on interminably, and fail to sustain the charges. There is downright supervisory cowardice to expose and punish the violence prone subordinates. Group solidarity triumphs over oath to honour the law and uphold the Constitution. National Police Commission recommended mandatory judicial enquiries in all cases of custodial deaths. In its annual reports, National Human Rights Commission (NHRC) mentions the compensation awarded to the victims by the Commission in cases of police torture and custodial deaths, but there is no indication of punishment imposed on the culpable officers. This is because in very few cases they are visited with exemplary punishment. Unbecoming conduct of the police is not the outcome of aberrations of some "bad apples". Police deviance is deep-seated. It is caused by an organisational culture that does not frown upon misuse and abuse of force and glorifies the ethic of masculinity. In many police training institutions, emphasis is still on hard-nosed and not humane policing. Human rights culture is yet to permeate the Indian police. Many police leaders forget the fact that indulgence in torture or other extra-legal strong arm tactics has a long-term corroding effect on the police organizations. It builds up "a guild of professional torturers" and work havoc with police professionalism. In cases of custodial deaths, the police have to contrive elaborate ingenuous device to cover their tracks. The police work ceases to be straightforward and a "bunker mentality" grows. It is also a fact that most of the victims of custodial torture are poor and disadvantaged people with little political or financial power to back them. Personal benefits, political considerations and, at times, pecuniary gains, become important considerations for custodial deaths, rather than investigation of cases. I have seen that human rights training and sensitisation of police officers and men have had just some marginal impact but more enduring result has been accomplished by constant exhortation by senior police leaders that custodial torture is illegal and counter-productive and will not be brooked.

5

Systemic Changes

A Must to Curb Fake Encounters

Encounter specialists continue to pose grave problems for the police administration and operations. Recently, a notorious encounter specialist of the Mumbai Police, Pradeep Sharma, was sentenced to life imprisonment by the Bombay High Court in a 2006 case. The Court also awarded a life sentence to 12 other cops, who were involved in the same case. This is exemplary punishment for trigger-happy police officers indulging in brazen illegalities.

However, the popular impression that fake encounters are the handiwork of errant cops is misleading. The hard fact to be acknowledged is that such encounters are the symptoms of a systemic malaise. At times, these encounters are staged by police officers because of the pressure exerted by their political masters and departmental bosses to show quick results by means fair or foul. The public, by and large, does not mind if cops take the law into their own hands and become executioners in the case of dreaded criminals.

The police dilemma is compounded by the slow-moving criminal justice system. As trials drag on indefinitely in the courts, witnesses are easily gained over or turn hostile. Hence, the police face tremendous pressure to adopt extrajudicial methods and shortcuts. Some civil libertarians presume that extrajudicial killings stem from the 'bloodthirstiness' of the police officials. This is not always the case. The police are encouraged to do the dirty work because the criminal justice system is not functioning properly, and overhauling the system is an arduous and time-consuming job.

But the fact to be constantly borne in mind is that encounters are counter-productive and encourage contempt for the law within the police. Breaking the law in the name of law enforcement is unacceptable in a democratic society governed by the rule of law. It is unacceptable because it is arbitrary as a process and random in effect.

In its report, the National Police Commission strongly condemned false encounters as a remedy. The need of the hour is to strengthen the law and legal processes. Unfortunately, some senior police officers, instead of resisting pressure from their political masters, bend over backwards to please them. As the DIG in charge of the Crime Investigation Department (CID) of the Odisha Police said, "I was berated by then Chief Minister for not knowing all the tricks of the 'police tradecraft'."

Admittedly, in every police department, there are violence-prone officers who frequently indulge in a disproportionate use of force. In the US, the Christopher Commission, which looked into the misuse of force by the police after the Rodney King incident (1991) in Los Angeles, could pinpoint a few officers who were frequently crossing a red line. There should be no hesitation on the part of the police leaders to discipline and, if necessary, weed out the black sheep.

Thus, for dealing with the menace of fake encounters, systemic changes are called for. The National Human Rights Commission (NHRC), on receiving complaints of false encounters from the Andhra Pradesh Civil Liberties Committee, held a public hearing in Hyderabad and recorded evidence. The NHRC Chairman, in a letter to the Chief Ministers, asked them to issue directions to all police stations through the Directors General of Police on procedures to be followed where deaths had occurred in encounters with the police. The Commission was of the view that the right to private defence should not be manipulated to justify fake encounters.

The procedure outlined by the NHRC laid down that in the case of an encounter in which the police were involved, immediate steps should be taken to investigate the facts and circumstances leading to the incident and ascertain how the offence was committed and by whom. Moreover, if officers belonging to the same police station are members of the encounter party, it would be appropriate that other police agencies, preferably the state CID, should take over the investigation of such cases. Unfortunately, these salutary instructions of the NHRC remain just on paper and are highlighted only in their breach. It is not known if the NHRC has taken firm and tangible measures to ensure that its mandatory instructions are acted upon.

In the Indian police, peer group supervision is also conspicuously missing, though it can be a powerful tool for ensuring accountability and all-round good policing. In Japan, police officers work in pairs with the understanding that one is responsible for the work and conduct of the other. Policemen work in groups in India also, but the ethos is against the assumption of mutual responsibility. Peer supervision is closer and better informed than supervision by senior officers, but, unfortunately, it has remained a neglected aspect of internal regulation.

Violating the rule of law in the name of law enforcement is not desirable even from the limited point of view of the police. There are instances where criminals have used the police to bump off their rivals in intra-gang warfare. A research study by a former DGP of Maharashtra has shown how the Mumbai Police used to help one group of criminals eliminate their rivals in fake encounters.

There are many in the police force who mistakenly believe that the end justifies the means. However, the adoption of impermissible means ultimately vitiates the end. Further, violating the rule of law has the effect of 'scapegoating' the police. Police officers, particularly the top brass, have to constantly remember that when the police take recourse to extra-legal methods to make up for the deficiencies of law and legal procedures, they are trying to remedy inadequacies which they did not create. American scholar David Bayley has aptly said: "Illegality in the service of public safety makes policing a furtive and anxious activity and undermines the pride, which is the basis of job satisfaction."

6

Decriminalising of More Offences the Way Forward

IT was reported recently that the Haryana Government will take a final call on the decriminalisation of offences under about 235 Acts. These will be treated as civil offences and covered by administrative measures and other non-criminal penalties.

Criminal sanctions have been traditionally viewed as society's moral condemnation of the defendant's behaviour and its "hatred, fear and contempt for the convict" (Henry M. Hart, *The Aims of Criminal Law*). Criminal sanction has thus a stigmatising quality. In view of the proliferation of criminal laws, it is strongly felt by some criminologists and law-enforcement experts that laws should be reviewed with the objective of decriminalisation of many aspects of human behaviour. Apart from crimes against persons and property, there are several offences which fall in the realm of immorality, such as gambling, liquor consumption, and sexual pursuits like pornography and prostitution.

It is also seen that many of these laws impinge upon individuals' freedom of action and are often either unenforceable or too costly to enforce. Norval Morris and Gordon Hawkins, in their book *The Honest Politician's Guide to Crime Control*, referred to the 'overreach' of the criminal law. They argued that the criminal justice system should be stripped of moralistic excrescences so that it can concentrate on the essential. Some criminologists opine that it is obligatory on the part of society to enforce morality through criminal sanctions. Conservative criminologists like H.L.A. Hart (Law, Liberty and Morality) and Patrick Devlin, however, believe that public morality is the 'cement of society', which must be maintained in order to prevent social disintegration. It is difficult to consider some kinds of behaviour as immoral when there is no consensus about their harmfulness.

It is also felt that decriminalisation, in a large measure, is necessary to reduce the workload on the police. The police are working under great stress and are plagued by the shortage of manpower and other material resources.

There is considerable substance in the argument of advocates of decriminalization that when the police are not able to devote adequate time to the investigation of important cases, they should not be burdened with probes into 'victimless' crimes.

The police are indeed devoting an enormous amount of time and energy to the investigation of such cases without getting proportionate results.

It is seen that many laws are criminogenic. Sometimes, laws create crimes by labelling and encouraging 'secondary deviance'. According to the labelling theory, the person who is arrested, prosecuted and convicted internalises the label of the criminal and proceeds to act out the role and commit crimes. The law also creates 'secondary deviance'. For instance, a drug addict takes to crime to keep up his habit because the drug is illegal and expensive.

Decriminalisation has been proposed in certain areas of criminal law. Some criminologists and law enforcement experts are of the view that sexual activities between consenting adults in private should not be the subject of criminal law in cases of adultery, homosexuality, pornography and obscenity. The Bharatiya Nyaya Sanhita (BNS), which will soon replace the Indian Penal Code (IPC), has omitted adultery as an offence. The Supreme Court decriminalised adultery in a landmark judgement in *Joseph Shine* vs.

Union of India (2018). The IPC's Section 497, which exempts the woman from culpability as an abettor and puts the entire blame on the man, is not part of the BNS. However, the new statute's Clause 84 has retained the IPC's Section 498, which penalises a man for enticing the wife of another man so that she may have intercourse with any person.

Under Section 377 of the IPC, homosexuality was both a non-cognisable and punishable offence. However, the Apex Court struck down Section 377 and decriminalised same-sex relations between consenting adults.

The BNS has dropped Section 309 (attempted suicide) of the IPC. However, attempted suicide with the intent of preventing a public servant from carrying out his/her duty is still a punishable offence.

Sections 292 and 293 of the IPC state that by itself, possession of obscene material is no offence unless it is so possessed for the purpose of sale, hire, distribution, public exhibition and circulation. Section 293 prohibits the sale of obscene material to any person under the age of 20. In 1969, Denmark became the first country in the world to legalise pornography. Initially, there was a great rush for obscene material, but soon the craze faded and people did not pay much attention to pornographic books and other material freely available for purchase. Similarly, perhaps, the time has come to think about decriminalisation of gambling by permitting it under licence. In Japan, law enforcement authorities focus on the activities of professional gamblers. No action is taken against betting for small sums of money. While decriminalising gambling, there should be essential safeguards; for example, no attempt must be made by people who indulge in gambling to use force or violence on anybody or entice juveniles into their group to further their activities.

The drug menace has become a malaise afflicting many countries. Like a tidal wave, illegal drugs are invading the global market. In the US, there is a growing feeling that criminalisation of heroin has done more harm than good. Advocates of decriminalisation acknowledge that the drug is a destructive commodity which requires control. Decriminalisation means the removal of criminal penalties for the use of heroin, but narcotic trafficking would remain a crime. Drug addiction should be viewed as a health-related rather than a criminal problem.

Similarly, cases registered under the liquor laws significantly increase the work on the police without solving the problem itself. There is a growing realisation that criminalisation is not an appropriate response to social and medical problems.

Constant efforts are needed to decriminalise unenforceable laws to ease the pressure on the justice delivery system.

7

Credibility Crisis of CBI

Move of the Central Bureau of Investigation (CBI) to close criminal proceedings against Ottavio Quattrocchi, has drawn flak from the Chief Metropolitan Magistrate, New Delhi. He criticised CBI's role in the investigation of the case against Quattrocchi and questioned its decision to approach Interpol for removal of the red corner notice against Quattrochi before obtaining court's permission for withdrawal of the case against him. Increasingly, CBI is losing credibility before the public as an independent investigating agency. This is a singularly unfortunate development that will seriously impede any meaningful efforts to combat corruption.

The CBI was set up under the Delhi Police Establishment Act (DPEA) in 1946. During its early years, the organization, under able and upright Directors, like D.P. Kohli, F. Arul enjoyed enviable reputation for transparency and professional competence. It selected its officers carefully and brooked no interference in its work. For IPS officers, deputation to the CBI was a prestigious assignment and they could function free from the pulls and pressures of the state politicians.

Decline of CBI and erosion of its credibility started during Emergency. The organization became politicized. The Shah

Commission of enquiry which looked into the excesses perpetrated during the emergency severely indicted the role of the CBI in a number of cases. In some cases, it came to light that it was acting *mala fide* and had become an instrument of harassment of innocent people. The then Director of CBI, D. Sen was an officer of great professional competence and inspired fear and awe from the subordinate staff. But he capitulated before the baleful pressures exerted by all powerful Sanjay Gandhi and his cronies and besmirched irretrievably the reputation of the organization. Shah Commission deplored the politicization of the organization and said that the fairness and objectivity with which an organization functions would in the ultimate analysis depend upon the extent to which the higher executives of the organization are allowed to function freely and objectively and at the same time ensuring their accountability to statutorily constituted bodies.

One of the main reasons for erosion of credibility of the CBI is political interference in its investigative functioning. Section 4 of the Delhi Police Establishment Act provides that CBI must function under the "superintendence" of the Central Government. Superintendence does not control or interference in the investigation conducted by CBI. In the case of Vineet Narain (1998), the Apex Court held that Section 4 cannot be construed so as to prevent actual supervision of the investigation of an offence by the CBI and the Central Government is precluded from issuing any direction to the CBI to curtail or inhibit its jurisdiction to investigate into offences.

Unfortunately, CBI has been functioning under successive Central Governments, as eminent jurist Fali Nariman has put it, "not by notes on files but on nods or winks" of the Minister or the senior bureaucrats in charge of the administrative Ministry. In cases of alleged corruption in the conduct of Commonwealth Games and handling up 2G spectrum by A. Raja, former Minister of Telecommunication, the CBI moved with disturbing slowness in taking necessary steps such as raids of houses of the officers and suspects, freezing their bank accounts, and their interrogation etc.

The public cannot be blamed if it draws adverse inferences. Now it has been directed to investigate the 2G Spectrum case under the supervision of the Apex Court. Unfortunately, in Vineet Narain's case (better known as Hawala Case) even under Court's scrutiny investigation was so inadequate, that charges could not be framed by the trial courts against the accused persons.

Indeed, much depends upon the mettle of the Director of the organization. He should be able to stand firmly against the nods and winks of the political masters. Now secure tenure of two years after selection as the Director, as enjoined by the court, gives him some elbow room. It is also the responsibility of the government to ensure, as the Shah Commission had recommended, that organizations like the CBI is led by competent self-respecting individuals, who are known for their appreciation of values and concern for the interests of the country and its citizens. "Lesser men as heads of such organization would only be a disaster."

Even now without extraneous interference, the CBI has done laudable investigation in cases relating to the assassination of Rajiv Gandhi in May 1991, and Mumbai's blasts of 1993 and in many other cases. Its performance has been acclaimed by all. To restore the credibility of CBI and make it an effective instrument for combating corruption there should be a comprehensive enquiry into the functioning of the CBI by an eminent professional of untarnished reputation or by a Joint Parliamentary Committee. The recommendations of such a committee have to be implemented in letter and spirit. At present, the annual reports of the working of the CBI's hardly figure in debates either in public or in Parliament. The CBI has to be insulated from extraneous pressures and made really independent. This has to be done by law expressly enacted by the Parliament. For this, there are models in other countries which can be suitably adapted.

There are suggestions that the Director of CBI like CAG could be given an independent constitutional status. Another alternative is to keep CBI under the Parliamentary control. The Parliament would oversee the functioning of the CBI either directly or through a committee. The CBI on the pattern of the Australian model could be made accountable and answerable to this committee as adapted to Indian conditions.

Nearer home Independent Commission Against Corruption (ICAC) set-up in Hong Kong has done a remarkable job in reducing corruption and enabling Hong Kong to break out of its corruption trap. The government indicated its commitment by appointing a person of unimpeachable integrity as the Chairman and prosecuting some big fish. There is need for strong political will to make CBI independent, apolitical and effective.

Another factor sapping the efficiency of the CBI is that its charter has been widened to deal with various other forms of crime not connected with corruption. It is saddled with all kinds of cases that have nothing to do with corruption. The strength of the CBI in order to make it an effective instrument has to be substantially augmented. In 1996, the Federal Bureau of Investigation had 11,400 investigating officers while the CBI had only 1,031. The Independent Commission Against Corruption (ICAC) whose activities are confined only to Hong Kong had as many as 684 investigators in its rolls. At present, CBI refuses to take over many cases but later on has to accept some of them either under court's orders or under the pressure of public opinion.

CBI's effective functioning suffers also because of constraints beyond its control. Monthly crime reports of CBI for the month of September 2010, indicated that on 30-9-2010 as many as 9,895 cases are pending for trial. Age-wise profile of the cases is the following:

Years	**Cases pending under Trial**
<2 years	2284
2 years–5 years	2475
5 years–10 years	2896
10 years–15 years	1190
15 years–20 years	645
>20 years	405
Total	**9895**

Source: Monthly Crimes Report of CBI of September 2010.

Again a number of cases are pending for prosecution sanction. As many as 108 cases are pending with Central Government departments/authorities and 24 cases pending with state governments for sanction. Prosecution sanction was ostensibly meant for a check against non-appreciation of departmental procedures by an investigating agency or the court. So the department was given the discretion. But the influential and the forceful can manage its denial (as shown in the case of P.J. Thomas) and frustrate the ends of justice. This provision needs to be removed from the statute.

8

Withdrawal of Communal Riot Cases in U.P. will be a Mistaken Step

The recent decision of the Government of Uttar Pradesh to initiate the process of withdrawal of cases linked to the 2013 Muzaffarnagar and Shamli communal riots is worrying, as it undermines effective and neutral policing and sends a wrong message to the family members of the victims. The communal riots in Muzaffarnagar and adjoining areas had claimed more than 60 lives and over 40,000 people were displaced. The communal carnage at Muzaffarnagar had shown how small incidents, if not firmly addressed in the beginning, snowball into violent communal confrontations. The gory communal riots exposed the culpability of the political leadership and incapacity, if not pusillanimity, of the police and district administration. The then-Chief Minister, Akhilesh Yadav, should have issued clear orders to the district administration to deal firmly with the situation and nip in the bud efforts of the interested groups to spread the communal fire. There were warning reports of the gathering storm. Intelligence agencies of the Central Government had issued warnings about the looming crisis, but no firm steps were taken to douse the communal flames.

For the failure to prevent communal riots in Muzaffarnagar, a major share of responsibility has to be borne by the police.

Though the communal riots may originate from many factors, over which the police have no control, failure of the police to act decisively and firmly leads to escalation of riots and consequent loss of lives and properties. In dealing with communal riots, the police will have to act firmly and swiftly and nab the anti-social elements, who take advantage of the situation and indulge in loot, arsons and murder. Nothing like this was done during riots at Muzaffarnagar. In such situations, one thumb rule is that senior police officers must take with a big pinch of salt the plea of the subordinates that anti-social elements have gone underground and could not be traced. A research study of the cases of stabbing during communal disturbances has shown that the stabbers were professional goons, and not the common men, or amateurs, acting on a sudden flash of communal frenzy. It is true that very often the police officers hesitate to take action because the hoodlums enjoy political patronage. Senior officers have to take a firm and no-nonsense stand against any political interference in tense law and order situations. Unfortunately, many are failing or faltering. I know the case of a Superintendent of Police, seeking clearance from the Chief Minister, before deciding to open fire on a riotous mob, and thereby allowing the situation to worsen.

It has been noticed that after gory communal riots in many states, the State governments have withdrawn cases against the persons charged with serious offences, on the plea of promoting communal harmony. Law Minister of UP, Brijesh Pathak, has said that the State government is considering withdrawal of cases which are "politically motivated". In most of these cases, the accused persons are charged with serious offences under the Indian Penal Code, like murder, attempt to commit murder and spreading communal hatred etc. Section 153 (A) of the IPC penalises the offence of promoting enmity between different groups, on grounds of race and religion. The offence is cognizable, non-bailable and punishable, with imprisonment up to five years. In my long innings in the police, I have seen very few cases of rioters being punished under this deterrent section. Withdrawal of criminal cases after communal riots, serves no purpose, and goes to encourage anti-social elements. The National Police Commission, in its report, has sternly deprecated this expedient measure and pointed out its undesirable fallouts. It endorsed the decision of the National Integration Council against withdrawal of such cases. A person indulging in acts of wanton violence, in the name of religion, should not be permitted to escape the rigours of law, only because he has influence in his own community, and is able to manipulate political support. The Law Minister of UP has said that the Government is thinking of withdrawing the cases because "they smacked of political vendetta".

The previous Government of Samajwadi Party had set up a special investigating team to investigate the communal riot cases. It should be left to the trial courts to decide on the truth of the matter, or otherwise, of the charges framed against the accused persons, some of whom are closely associated with the ruling party. Withdrawal of cases will engender fear and anguish among the victims, and reflect poorly on the neutrality of the state administration. Ongoing debate on the incidence of communal riots during the previous Samajwadi Party regime, and the present BJP dispensation, serves no purpose. It is true that riots of more graver nature and intensity had taken place during the SP regime, but the litmus test is the prevalence of a sense of security and safety among the members of minority communities. Here, Adityanath government also fails.

Section 321 of the Criminal Procedure Code grants the public prosecutor the leeway to withdraw from prosecution any person, either generally, or in respect of anyone, or more, of the offences for which he is tried, with the consent of the court. Withdrawal of cases has to be authorised by the state government. But the State government is not free to exercise its authority in a whimsical and arbitrary manner, or for extraneous considerations. Unfortunately, very often, extraneous political considerations influence decisions of the State government. But parameters for withdrawal must withstand judicial scrutiny, and the courts should not permit withdrawal of cases filed by the public prosecutor, without rigorous scrutiny.

The Supreme Court has laid down in the case of *Ramnarain Pandey* v. *State of Bihar* that the court has to satisfy itself that the executive function of the prosecution has not been improperly exercised, or it is not an attempt to interfere with the normal course of justice for illegitimate reasons and purposes.

Unfortunately, convictions in cases of communal riots are few. Seldom the miscreants receive deterrent punishment. In Uttar Pradesh, acquittal of all the accused persons in the 1987 Hasimpura massacre, in which 41 persons (all Moslems), were shot dead in cold blood by the personnel of the UP Armed Constabulary, was a shocking miscarriage of justice. Withdrawal of cases gives the accused persons a feeling that, with political backing, they can cock a snook at the criminal justice machinery of the state. This will deepen the sense of anger and alienation of the victims, most of whom belong to the minority community. They will tend to lose faith, not only in the forces of law and order, but in the government itself, and turn to narrow obscurantist groups and not mainstream political parties to represent their sectarian interests. And this bodes ill for the country.

9

Lawless Policing is an Abomination in a Free Society

In a democratic society, the law vests vast powers in the hands of the police to curb lawlessness by anti-social elements, but also keeps provisions to ensure that these powers are not used to imperil the rights of citizens. The conviction of criminals is important, but more important is the fact that the police must function in a way that promotes the values of a liberal, democratic society.

(Illegal means ultimately undermine the ends. This approach damages the credibility of the police—Sankar Sen Ex-Director, National Police Academy). The basic functions of the police include law enforcement and maintenance of order. But often it is witnessed that in the rough and tumble of policing for the sake of maintaining and enforcing order, the police violate rules and norms of laws, leading to lawlessness and dishonest enforcement of laws.

This conundrum in law enforcement was driven home to me by the then Chief Justice of the Orissa High Court, R.L. Narasimham. At that point, I was posted as Assistant Superintendent of Police in Cuttack. While discussing law and order problems of Cuttack city, Justice Narasimham stated that the police have to constantly bear in mind that order has to be maintained through law; otherwise, dacoits can ensure better order than the police any day. It was a very perceptive observation.

The British rulers tried to build up the Indian police on the pattern of the Army. The Indian Police Act of 1861 was enacted after the 'Sepoy Mutiny' of 1857 as the foreign rulers wanted to set up a loyal and pliant police force. The *khaki* uniform and badges of ranks were similar to those of the Army and there was overemphasis on drill, parade and physical fitness.

Thus, during our training as probationers at the Central Police Training College in Mount Abu, we were constantly told that the police service was neither meant for the weak and faint-hearted nor for people with utopian thoughts and ideas. War against crime is hard and relentless — almost a Sisyphean task, meant for the tough and flint-hearted.

During my first posting in the district, the SP, a rough-hewn and weather-beaten police officer, bluntly told me to bury five fathoms deep what had been taught in the training school and adjust quickly to the stark ground realities. There were many other senior officers like him who echoed a similar view: that in policing, the ends justify the means.

In order to see that criminals and lawless elements get their just deserts, rules and laws, if necessary, have to be bent. For a firm and effective policing, a police officer should not confine himself to the four corners of the law. There is also public demand and pressure on the police to adopt shortcuts and third-degree methods with a view to punishing the hardened and dreaded criminals, who cock a snook at the prevailing and slow-moving criminal justice system.

However, illegality in the name of law enforcement is an anachronism that perverts the system and coarsens the law enforcement officers. Any monstrous act of police violence or atrocity generates police phobia and turns public anger against the police. Many laudable and courageous deeds of the police are forgotten and their follies and foibles are highlighted. The police also become the scapegoats for the deficiencies of other agencies of the criminal justice system.

Deprived of solicitude from the public and media, they develop a fortress mentality and see the world as "we" and "they". Criminologist Gordon Misner, while explaining the police psychology, says policemen view themselves as "crime fighters standing against the Mongol hordes without the support of the public, politicians and the courts." Even many conscientious police officers feel that they are doing a difficult and dangerous job without any understanding by the society of their moral and professional problems.

Research studies have shown that the denigration by the public and press have an unsettling impact on the police morale. In fact, the police violence and brutality, as political scientist and criminologist David Bayley says, are often correlated to the public regard for the police authority. Low public regard reduces the self-esteem of the police and, thereby, they make use of force more often. On the other hand, unwarranted use of force lowers public regard for the police. It is also seen that the misuse or excessive use of force is restricted in societies where reserve and physical restraints are valued.

This is a cultural variable. Bailey, in his book, *Forces of Order: Police Behaviour in Japan and the United States*, says in Japan, a policeman who forbears the use of force even at the risk of severe emotional repression is respected for doing so. In contrast, in the US, policemen cannot allow challenges to their authority go unmet. Backing down is considered cowardly in India. The military model of policing still continues, largely unchanged. There is a far greater emphasis on discipline and strict maintenance of order than on service to the people and upholding their rights.

In a democratic society, the law vests vast powers in the hands of the police to curb lawlessness by anti-social elements, but also keeps provisions to ensure that these powers are not used to imperil the rights of the citizens. The conviction of criminals is important, but more important is the fact that the police must function in a way that promotes the values of a liberal, democratic society. Illegal and impermissible means ultimately undermine the ends.

The absence of a human rights culture also prompts the police to adopt impermissible means for the maintenance of order. The quintessence of human rights is respect for human dignity, and in India, the policemen are yet to learn to respect the rights and dignity of the minorities, women and marginalised sections of society. They often become the targets of abuse of force and violence by the police. The mandate of the police to use force to curb violence and lawlessness raises the key issue that the police themselves should not indulge in unnecessary or excessive use of force. Lawless policing becomes an abomination in a free society.

Again, lawless policing is not desirable from a practical point of view. I have witnessed many promising careers of young police officers coming to a sad end for transgressing laws and perpetrating illegalities due to the mistaken notion that the ends justifies the means and "noble cause corruption" is necessary and unavoidable. But the truth is that the adoption of illegalities damages the standing and credibility of the police and erodes their effectiveness. They forfeit public cooperation and without its support, it is not possible to effectively control public disorder.

The Independent Commission on Policing in Northern Ireland (Patten Commission) has aptly said, "Bad application or promiscuous use of the power to limit a person's human rights by such means as arrest, strip and search and house searches can lead to bad police relations with the entire neighbourhood, thereby rendering in effect policing of those neighbourhood impossible."

Former Chief Justice Narasimham's observation on maintenance of order through law should be borne in mind by every police officer. It underscores the essence of law enforcement and provide a valuable insight into the core functions of the police.

10

Landmark SC Ruling Targets Menace of Child Marriage

In a landmark decision, the Supreme Court of India has issued a slew of directives to the Centre and State governments to eradicate the heinous social evil of child marriage. The Apex Court has also ordered the creation of special police units to firmly address the cancerous evil across the country.

However, the challenge is daunting. Child marriage is an age-old social evil that has a long history. Various factors, such as social cultural and economic, are responsible for the need to protect unmarried girls from the covetous eyes of foreign invaders. Hence, early marriage of the children was preferred and later on, became a rigid social custom. The Problem was further compounded by the dowry system. The fear of payment of heavy dowry for the marriage of a girl after puberty, made the practice common, particularly among the poor and economically weaker sections of the society. In the rural areas of some states, if the girl is not married before she has attained the age of 17 years, the entire family is ostracised.

It is aptly said that child marriage is an "evil more grave than *Sati* because it is more devastating in its consequences and more insidious in its workings." For the girl, it leads to inadequate socialisation, discontinuation of education and great physiological damages owing to repeated pregnancy. There is evidence to support that the maximum maternal deaths take place between 15 to 16 years of age, when a girl is no longer a child and yet unprepared for marriage.

Under the Child Marriage Restraint Act (after its amendment in 1978) the minimum legal marriage is 18 years for women and 21 years for men. The Child Marriage Restraint Act was a legislative Act passed on 28 September, 1929. The Act fixed the marriageable age for girls at 14 years and 18 years for boys. It is popularly known as the Sharda Act after its sponsor Harbilas Sharda.

The Prohibition of Child Marriage Act, 2006 replaced the 1929 Act with the same minimum age limits. The Prohibition of Child Marriage (Amendment) Bill makes the age of marriage for females to 21 years.

The Social Development Council, New Delhi, conducted a study of child marriages in Rajasthan and Andhra Pradesh and concluded that this piece of legislation has remained a dead letter because of the prevalent social and religious customs, poor economic conditions and ineffective enforcement machinery. Although the prescribed age limit for the marriage of girls is 18, hundreds of young girls are married on the occasion of *Akshaya Tritiya* in Rajasthan as well as in some parts of Bihar, Andhra Pradesh and Tamil Nadu.

The Social Development Council conducted a study of social marriages in Rajasthan and Andhra Pradesh and concluded that this piece of legislation to prevent child marriage remained a dead letter because of the prevalent social customs, poor economic conditions, inadequate vocational employment and ineffective enforcement machinery. Another study conducted by the Council of Social Development for the Ministry of Social Welfare, Government of India, has dealt with the perception of women themselves on the issue of child marriage. Many women look on early marriage as protection against sexual molestation. Again, when a girl grows up, it is difficult to get a suitable match and dowry demand also goes up. Further, child marriage is actually a betrothal as '*gauna*' or real marriage takes place when the girl is much older. Discussions with women also reveal another negative side of the issue. Boys, who marry early, have a tendency to abandon their wives and get remarried when they grow older.

Meanwhile, after publication of a news item in an English daily that marriage on a large scale will be solemnised in Rajasthan on April 29,1998, the day of *Akshaya Tritiya*, the National Human Rights Commission issued a notice to the Chief Secretary of Rajasthan and called for a detailed report to know the action taken by the State Government to prevent child marriages. It also sent a team for an on-the-spot probe. Senior officers visited Bikaner and Jodhpur and witnessed a number of child marriages being solemnised with great fanfare and without any objection from the authorities or members of the public.

The Commission pointed out to the State government that it was a statutory obligation on its part under the Child Marriage Restraint Act to prevent child marriages and take appropriate action in accordance with the provisions of the Act and also called for a report from the Rajasthan government on the prevalence of child marriages in the state.

11

Impeachment of the Chief Justice of India

A Black Day for Indian Judiciary

Rejection of the Congress led opposition's notice for the removal of the Chief Justice of India by the Chairman, Rajya Sabha Venkaiya Naidu marks another turn in the unedifying drama of impeachment of the Chief Justice of the Apex Court. The Chairman, Rajya Sabha, rejected the notice on the ground that the charges were neither "tenable nor sustainable". This is for the first time such a notice was rejected by the Chairman of the House at the first stage.

Many eminent jurists and legal eagles of the country like Soli Sorabjee and Fali Nariman have clearly expressed the view that the impeachment move was ill-conceived and politically motivated. Nariman feels that it is the "blackest day" in the annals of the Indian judiciary. He also expressed fear that it would tarnish the image of the judiciary and would provide a handle to the ruling party to initiate similar moves for removal of judges whose judgements it did not like.

The ball was set rolling when earlier four seniormost judges of the Supreme Court in an open press conference criticised the Chief Justice of India for assigning important cases to favoured panels of judges by overriding the principle of seniority. It was an unprecedented event that the Chief Justice of the Supreme Court was accused of acting arbitrarily in assigning key cases, such as the mysterious death of Justice B.H. Loya, and provided an opening to the political parties to bring the notice for CJI's removal. The impeachment motion was perhaps the direct result of the press conference.

Charges listed by the opposition lack substance and have very little to do with judicial functions. A well-known jurist has called them frivolous and trumped up. Finance Minister Arun Jaitley is justified in calling it a "revenge petition". The Congress knows that no enquiry against the CJI will end by the time he demits office in October this year. It also knows that it lacks strength in the Parliament to succeed. Its main ulterior aim, therefore, is to compel the CJI to recuse. Hence, perhaps, it is more a recusal motion than an impeachment motion. One of the allegations against the CJI relates to acquisition of land even before his elevation as a judge of the High Court. Incidentally, it was the Congress government which appointed him as a judge in 1996. He became the Chief Justice of the Patna High Court and finally elevated to the Supreme Court in 2011. Two other charges relate to intra-court functioning and assignment of cases. The main ground for the opposition is the fifth and last point of allocation of cases to the judges. Well-known jurists like Fali Nariman and Soli Sorabjee are of the clear view that the CJI is the Master of the Roster, and allocation of cases cannot be a ground for impeachment. The CJI cannot be impeached simply because some people, and even some judges, disagree with his calls.

It is imperative that the grounds for impeaching the Chief Justice of the country must be extraordinarily grave and serious. There has to be iron-clad grounds for the alleged misbehaviour on the part of the CJI. The Chief Justice and Judges of the Supreme Court are the final interpreters of the Constitution and impeaching them on unsustainable grounds amount to attempts at destroying the Constitution. The independence of the judiciary will be at stake. The move has generated considerable noise and heat in the media and has gone to undermine the moral authority of the judiciary. The view of the Rajya Sabha Chairman that considering the totality of facts, it is neither legal nor desirable to admit the notice of impeachment.

The not-so-hidden agenda of the Congress is to delay the hearing of the *Babri Masjid case* for which Kapil Sibal had earlier made fervent pleas in the court. The Congress wants the CJI to recuse from this case. There is no constitutional provision for recusal on filing of, or admission of a motion for impeachment. In the case of the Supreme Court Judge, Veeraswamy, the then Chief Justice of the Supreme Court, had withdrawn judicial work from him after the Lok Sabha Speaker admitted the motion against him and set up an enquiry committee headed by the Supreme Court Judge Chenappa Reddy, which later found Veeraswamy guilty of most of the charges of corruption.

Fali Nariman is of the clear opinion that the opposition parties have not carefully considered all aspects of the matter before taking the plunge. A righteous man like the former Prime Minister Manmohan Singh did not sign the notice because he must have felt that impeachment provisions must not be abused for scoring cheap political points. Kapil Sibal's points that, as the former Prime Minister, he should be kept above the din of controversy, does not wash.

Indeed, impeachment controversy has given a body blow to the image of the Indian judiciary. During discussions, a retired Chief Justice of the Supreme Court told me that it is imperative for the Supreme Court Judges to step forward to heal the rift and set the things right. The lack of collegiality among the judges of the Apex Court, which has openly surfaced, is a threat to the aura and respect for Indian judiciary. Some urgent corrective steps are called for. Fali Nariman has suggested that the four judges, who earlier wrote the letter of January 12, may say that they were not a party to subscribing any charge against the Chief Justice warranting impeachment. Justice J. Chelameswar, the prime mover behind the January 12 Press Conference, expressed the view that removal of a judge was not a solution to the issues facing the judiciary.

The Chairman of the Rajya Sabha has said that he exercised his discretion as a constitutional functionary, in conformity of the provisions of the Constitution, after “due diligence”.

The Congress plans to challenge the Rajya Sabha Chairman’s rejection of the impeachment petition in the Supreme Court. It held the Chairman’s decision as ill-advised and hasty. But the legal experts are of the clear view that the power to accept or decline the motion is a part of the legislative process of Parliament and exercise of discretion by the Chair of either House is not justiciable in the court of law. It is entirely for the Speaker/Chairman of the respective House to have come to the conclusion to accept or reject the motion.

12

Non-criminalisation of Marital Rape is Patriarchal and Unequal

In an affidavit before the Supreme Court, the Union Government has taken a stand against criminalisation of marital rape. In the affidavit before the Apex Court, the Home Ministry mentioned that a man has no fundamental right to force sex on his wife as there were enough laws to protect women against sexual violence and as such criminalisation of marital rape will be an extremely "harsh measure".

The Supreme Court is hearing a number of petitions seeking to amend the British era law that a man cannot be prosecuted for rape within marriage, even though violence within marriage is rampant in India. According to a recent government survey, one in every twenty-five women has faced sexual violence from their husbands. In January 2023, the Supreme Court appointed two advocates as nodal counsels to streamline the proceedings by compiling a common document of relevant materials from all parties.

Currently, marital rape is outlawed in more than hundred countries in the world. It was outlawed in Great Britain in 1991. India is one of the few countries, along with Pakistan, Afghanistan and Saudi Arabia, where, marital rape law remains in force.

The Indian government in its affidavit, highlighted the fact that the parliament in its wisdom has deliberately chosen to retain the marital rape exception and urges the court to defer to legislative judgement in such sensitive matters. The parliament is directly elected by the people and is aware of the understanding of the people in such delicate sensitive issues. In the affidavit, the government urged the court to exercise judicial restraint and leave the regulation of marital relations to the wisdom of the parliament.

A number of petitions have been filed by different women's rights groups to strike down Section 375 of the IPC, which mentions several situations, in which having sex is not considered as rape. One of them being sex by a man with his wife, if she is not a minor.

According to the campaigners, this kind of argument is medieval and unacceptable in modern times. The United Nations, Human Rights Watch and Amnesty International have raised concerns about India's refusal to criminalise marital rape.

The Delhi High Court has given a split verdict, which remains pending for the Supreme Court's final judgement, where one judge has held that marital rape is "morally repugnant" and the other expressed the view that exception to 375 IPC is valid and should continue to exist. It has to be borne in mind that the marital exception to the IPC, and definition of marital rape was drafted on the basis of Victorian norms that did not recognise men and women are equal and merged the identity of husband and wife under the "Doctrine of coverture".

Further, the marital rape violates the right to equality enshrined in the Article 14 of the Constitution of India. Hence, it creates two classes of women based on their marital status and immunises action perpetrated by men against their wives. There is no other reason for victimisation of women other than their married status. Moreover, it becomes difficult for married women to avoid abusive conditions because of their financial dependence on their husbands. The exemption is also violative of Article 21 of the Constitution, which includes right to life and encompasses right to health, privacy and dignity. The Supreme Court has recognised the right to abstain from sexual activity for all women, irrespective of their marital status as a fundamental right guaranteed by the Constitution.

In 2013, the United Nations Committee on Elimination of Discrimination Against Women (CEDAW) strongly recommended that the Government of India should criminalise marital rape. The forthcoming judicial review by the Apex Court will provide an opportunity to eliminate a discriminatory legal relic that violates the fundamental rights in the Constitution and will help to transform women's lives and rights.

However, opponents of criminalising marital rape, including the government, argue that it would threaten the sanctity of family life, increase false allegations, disrupt marital harmony and undermine the institution of marriage itself. But these arguments seem to be presumptions, meant to smoke screen the harsh realities faced by countless women.

Section 2

13

Truce in Gaza

Relentless bombing of Gaza by Israel has wrought havoc. According to Palestinian health officials more than several thousand civilians have been killed due to indiscriminate Israeli bombing and many of them are women and children. Hospitals are also being bombed on the ground that the Hamas terrorists have taken shelter and set up their underground operation centres there.

As a result, the patients, including those critically injured, are going without treatment. The Director General of WHO has described the situation as "dire and perilous" and said that because of shortage of fuel, very soon the humanitarian operations will come to a grinding halt. The most difficult phase of Israeli operations against the Hamas has now commenced. The Israeli Army has encircled Gaza city and divided the enclave into two parts. Finishing off the Hamas will be a bloody and tough job. Hamas has built up 300 miles of tunnels, where it stores its military possessions and these tunnels cannot be destroyed by aerial bombardment. Like the Vietcong guerrillas of Vietnam in the 1960s, Hamas has built a wide network of tunnels that are fully self-contained.

The Israeli army will be very hesitant to send its soldiers inside the tunnels because of fear of heavy casualties and will keep their operations over ground, as much as possible. Night vision devices and communication tools which rely on satellites will not work underground. The Israeli army will try to destroy the tunnels by bulldozing their entries or exits or filling them with sea water. But the possibility of hostages being kept in tunnels will slow down the Israeli response. There are intelligence reports that hostages are actually being kept in tunnels. There will be street to street fighting.

Hamas has almost 40,000 tough street fighters, who will resort to ambushes and hit-and-run tactics. Hamas says that claims made by the Israeli Defence Force (IDF) are illusionary and already several hundred Israeli soldiers and officers have been killed in ambushes. According to the *Wall Street Journal*, the arsenal of Hamas has improved over the years and includes drones, rockets, grenades and Iranian made surface-to-air missiles. According to a Hamas spokesman, the group has already set up factories producing these arms. There is a difference of opinion among experts if IDF is capable of destroying the military capabilities of Hamas. Some feel that IDF can do so.

But there is now growing international pressure on Israel to halt its military operations in Gaza and desist from collective punishment of the civilians there. The civil society across the world has staged protests against Israel. Many Jews in America have also joined the peace campaigns. Prime Minister Benjamin Netanyahu has already acted on his statement that Israel is open to "tactical little pauses" in Gaza fighting to facilitate the entry of humanitarian aid or allow the exit of hostages held by Hamas. But there will be no general ceasefire. Netanyahu is facing strong domestic criticism for failure to get the hostages released.

Thus, the two main goals of Israel—to completely neutralise Hamas militarily and ideologically and get the hostages released early—are colliding with each other. Israel may be constrained to cut a deal with the Hamas for release of the hostages. It is also very unlikely that harsh collective punishment of the Palestinians will decimate the Hamas leadership. Some of its leaders have already taken shelter in Oman and some others have escaped to Iran or Lebanon. Iran and the pro-Iranian militant group Hezbollah in

Lebanon support Hamas. Hamas has already announced that some of the hostages have been killed due to Israeli bombing.

Netanyahu was for some time working under the expectation that Israel could normalise its ties with the Arab world without addressing the Palestinian question, which he believed could be wished away. Now, the Palestinian question has again come to the forefront and can no longer be ignored. Saudi Arabia, which was on the verge of normalising relations with Israel, will demand more concessions for the Palestinians before moving forward lest it incurs the ire of its population and the wider Arab world. Netanyahu has said that Israel will remain in charge of the security of Gaza for an indefinite period.

Neither Washington nor Israel is yet very clear about Gaza's future. The US Secretary of State, Antony Blinken said to CBS Television that Hamas has to be dismantled but Israel cannot reoccupy Gaza and put the clock back. But without a ready replacement of Hamas, Israel will have little choice but to assume direct control over Gaza. This step, however, will exacerbate Palestinian militancy, deepen the divisions within Israeli society and tie up its military-economic resources in open-ended counter insurgency campaigns.

The United Nations Security Council has passed a resolution calling for urgent and expanded humanitarian pauses and unconditional release of the hostages. The USA did not block the resolution, but Israel criticised it for being "disconnected from reality". President Joe Biden has said that the end point of the Israel-Hamas conflict will be a Palestinian state that is real, and exists alongside Israel.

There are Israeli leaders who support the view that Palestinian authorities who cooperate with Israel in the administration of the Israeli-occupied West Bank should take charge of Gaza. There is, however, the danger that if the Palestinian Authority returns on the back of an Israeli invasion, it will be viewed by the Palestinians as the enemy. Now a ceasefire in the war between Israel and Hamas brokered by Qatar is on.

Hostages have been released by Hamas, and Israel in turn has freed Palestinian prisoners. With the truce deal come increased shipments of fuel and aid supplies to Gaza. Netanyahu says that he will continue vigorously with the war once the ceasefire comes to an end. Abu Ubalda, spokesperson of the Hamas armed wing, has also called it a temporary truce. It is hoped that international pressure will prevail and the truce will not be a shortlived one.

14

The Afghan Cauldron

Terror and violence in Afghanistan continue unabated. Nearly 200 people have been killed in the past month in deadly suicidal attacks perpetrated by the Taliban. Afghan authorities claim these outrages were masterminded by terrorists based and trained in Pakistan.

This is confirmed by the confessions of some of the captured ISIS militants. Pakistan, as usual, has denied the charge and alleged that Afghanistan is providing safe haven to the terrorists and other insurgents. The fighting usually abates during winter, but this year the Taliban and Islamic State groups have intensified their operations in response to US air assaults.

Earlier, President Trump had bluntly criticised Pakistan for providing support to the terrorists particularly the Haqqani network whose activists are killing American troops in Afghanistan.

Many in the US view Pakistan as the biggest disruptive force in Afghanistan. But this is the first time an American President has advanced such a stern message. At a meeting of the National Security Council, President Trump stated that the US has given Pakistan $ 33 billion over the past 15 years, but in turn has been deceived by Pakistan.

America has already cut off security-related assistance to Pakistan and has threatened to take more drastic steps if Pakistan does not change its course. There is little likelihood of any major shift in Pakistan's policy under American pressure. In an article in *Foreign Affairs*, Sumit Ganguly and Christian Fair have written: "After much puffery, the Trump administration has sent an unequivocal message to a duplicitous ally. Even if this does not change Pakistan's behaviour, the American public will have the satisfaction of knowing that they are no longer subsidising a country that undermines its regional interest in every conceivable way." Another columnist David Rhode, writing in *New Yorker*, remarked that "Pakistan has been a Frankenstein's monster for decades but this diplomatic gun-slinging will end up benefitting China".

Earlier American efforts to exert pressure on Pakistan to change its policy of covertly supporting the non-state actors in Afghanistan had not been successful. In 2011, President Obama suspended the $800 million assistance package and the Congress blocked the sale of F-16 fighters to Pakistan. None of these measures worked. Now the Pakistan army appears to have pushed the Haqqani network from Miran Shah, North Waziristan's capital, to the lightly monitored frontier.

But the Pakistani generals are not willing to squeeze them any further as they fear that more pressure on the Afghan militants might trigger domestic blowbacks. There are other security considerations as well. The Pakistan army views unfriendly Afghanistan as a major security threat. Pakistan was one of the very few countries to recognise the Taliban regime as it felt that it would be friendly to Pakistan's security interests based on the existential fear of India.

Michael Kugelman, Deputy Director of Programme Asia in Wilson Centre, has pointed out that Pakistan has deep immutable strategic interests that entail maintaining ties with the Talibans.

This explains why Pakistan has not taken any determined action against the Haqqani network. It has hummed and hawed, offering up now and then some low-level Haqqani operatives and occasionally trimming the support available to them.

President Trump's comment that India must have a larger footprint in Afghanistan is deeply worrying for Pakistan. Pakistani Generals fear that India, with Afghanistan as a base, will meddle in Pakistan and support the rebels in Baluchistan. Hence, Pakistan will continue to support the Haqqanis and other groups that bolster its interest of keeping India at bay in Afghanistan. Pakistani Generals are livid at American bullying.

They realise that they hold the trump card and can stop American supplies to the NATO forces and the Afghan government through Pakistan. The other alternative route will be longer and require Russian consent—not an easy arrangement. However, America can tighten the screws on Pakistan in many ways. It happens to be the biggest export market for Pakistan. Pakistani-Americans form one of its major diaspora groups. Ryan Crocker, former American ambassador in Pakistan and Afghanistan, has said in a CNN interview that President Trump must make it clear that American troops will continue its operations in Afghanistan and help the Afghan army till some settlement is reached.

Further, it will not refrain from pursuing and striking at the Taliban even inside Pakistan. The hard fact is that without American support, the Afghan army and security forces will not be able to withstand the fire and fury of the Taliban. President Ghani has also acknowledged that if American troops are now withdrawn, the present Afghan regime will collapse.

In the US military's semi-annual assessment to Congress in June, General John Nicholson Jr., Commander of US Forces, said the Taliban's exploitation of ungoverned sanctioned sanctuaries outside of Afghanistan (aka Pakistan) "is the single greatest external factor that could cause failure of the coalition campaign."

In addition to US troops, NATO and its alliance partners have more than 6,500 troops in the theatre. The Afghan National Army numbers about 1,75,000 including the Afghan Air force. Government forces suffer from poor leadership in some areas, a lack of care for those wounded or killed, inconsistent pay, and training and inadequate living conditions.

President Ashraf Ghani has agreed to a four-year plan to reinvent the Afghan military by expanding its special forces and Air Force with continued American support. The plan envisions large-scale manoeuvres in 2020 to break the stalemate with the Taliban. The situation in Afghanistan has been further compounded by the turf war between the Taliban and ISIS insurgents.

Reports indicate that fighters owning allegiance to the Islamic State succeeded in capturing large territories from the Taliban in Nanghar province of Afghanistan which borders Pakistan. ISIS fighters are mainly the disaffected Taliban activists, disillusioned by the movement's failure to return to power in Kabul. Black flags of the ISIS have been hoisted in some of the captured areas. Thus, its intervention introduces a new dimension to the Afghan war.

Rising levels of violence and the Caliphate's rapid growth in Afghanistan should set alarm bells ringing in Pakistan. Last year, it perpetrated one of the deadliest suicide attacks in Pakistan. Along with terrorist violence, opium cultivation has increased in Afghanistan. The UN Drug Report of 2014 states that the country produced 85 per cent of the world's opium. Eradication programmes target the poor farmers and not the influential poppy growers. Many farmers stripped of their livelihood joined the Taliban.

Among the regional powers, China is concerned because Uighur separatists are receiving military training and acquiring experience in Afghanistan. There are also economic and political considerations. China's Silk Route Economic Belt strategy is geared to develop infrastructure that will connect Eurasian economies, giving China better access to new markets. Being a close ally of Pakistan, China can bridge the gap between Pakistan and Afghanistan.

Trump has calculated that as long as he keeps Afghanistan from blowing up or sliding into civil war like Iraq, he can afford to keep US troops engaged without paying too high a domestic political price, according to Shibley Telhami, a pollster and professor at the University of Maryland. The risk is that there will be a sharply higher rate of US casualties that would shape America's public opinion of the 17-year conflict.

America will have to work through diplomacy with other countries, especially China and Gulf Arab states that share US concern about Pakistan's tolerance of terrorist organisations and individuals. While China will avoid steps that embarrass Pakistani leaders or that significantly skew the two countries' historically close ties, Beijing may be willing to work with Washington behind the scenes to press Pakistan to crack down on terrorists within its territory. Gulf countries, too, must be encouraged to press Pakistan to change its direction.

15

China's Road Ahead

Well-known columnist Farid Zakaria observed in an article published in *Newsweek* some time back that the 21st century belongs to China. From a third world nation, China has now risen as the second most important country on the planet. In 1990, China was just like any third world country with a per capita income of less than three dollars a day. After the crackdown in Tiananmen Square, China had to put on hold its economic policies and programmes. There were loud criticisms from Western countries of suppression of human rights in China. But Chinese leader Deng Xiao Ping boldly decided to continue with economic reforms and not to freeze them. He made the famous observation that "one does not stop eating for fear of choking." The rest is history. During the next three decades, China's growth was ten per cent a year and it emerged as the second largest economy in the world. It carried on industrialisation at breakneck speed and achieved in the course of one generation "what it took Europe three hundred years to achieve." Zakaria notes that this rapid and almost miraculous transformation was achieved with remarkable lack of violence. It is said dismissively by some critics that this had been possible because of the totalitarian regime in China. But so were many countries of the West when they were industrialised.

The spectacular economic growth has released tremendous energy which has been diffused all over the country. The boom thus has many legs. China has succeeded in pulling nearly 450 million people out of poverty. This perhaps is the greatest poverty reduction programme in human history. There is justifiable national pride at the country's rapid economic development and modernisation. There is also anger against the West, and particularly the United States, for its containment strategy against China. The Chinese Communist Party projects itself as the defender of the country's honour and presents the West as "an evil force". Riding high on nationalism, China is very critical of the West but is pragmatic enough to avoid any serious confrontation with it. America and the West are the main export market of China and the main providers of science and technology. The USA and the European Union account for 50 per cent of Chinese exports. But, bashing of the West will continue as it enables Chinese leaders to distract popular attention from pressing domestic issues. Aggressive nationalism in turn is leading to growing authoritarianism in China. President Xi Jing Ping is now vested with untrammelled power and authority. He is the president, party chief and the head of the armed forces. There is erosion of leadership among the equals which Deng had created to prevent authoritarianism of one person. However, China's growth is now slowing down to 5 per cent and recent studies show that there will be substantial growth slowdown due to demographic decline, limits of capital intensive growth and a gradual deceleration in productivity growth. It may slow down to 3 per cent by 2030. Even with this growth rate, China would become the world's largest economy but would never enjoy a meaningful lead over the United States. In the 20th party Congress, Xi got an unprecedented third five-year term as the party president and tightened his grip over the party and the army. He also filled up the Politburo standing committee with hardcore loyalists. He also asserted that China will not hesitate to use force and other powers necessary for reunification of Taiwan. Under him the CPC has become a one leader party and he is now endeavouring to make China a one leader country. He plans and promises to restore by mid-century the lost glory and status of the Middle Kingdom. Under Xi, China is aggressively converting herself into a hyper nationalist state determined to win back its lost exalted status. It is trying to browbeat its neighbours to submission in the South China Sea. It is projecting aggressively its extensive maritime claims by militarising islands. And the county is setting up a high tech surveillance structure, including a social credit system to control social behaviour of the citizens. This is creating a huge challenge for the international order and hastening a Cold War like situation. For decades America has bought more goods from China than it has sold to the country. This has led to mounting American debt and China's staggering trade surplus of $370 billion. If China offloads a substantial portion of its dollar reserves, it can bring the currency crashing down with devastating consequences for the United States. Today, China is asserting itself because of the economic strength it has acquired. This was done slowly and imperceptibly over a long period of time and America did not grasp it. It thought that it was living in an unchanging world. But the world around it did change. A global power has to develop economic muscle and not just talk tough. But China is also facing serious problems. Besides the problem of massive corruption, China has the problem of an eroding workforce. George Shambaugh, a well-known China expert and a professor in Georgetown university has argued that China is in a state of decline and this will continue if no major political reforms take place in the near future. XI's ruthless measures will bring the country to the breaking point. But these reforms are not going to take place because the Communist regime in China is unsure and can only think in terms of control and coercion. Thus, China is in no position to challenge the global hegemony of the United States. There are scholars who believe that America and China are on a collision course and this is against the background of the escalating tariff war between the two countries. President Trump imposed heavy import duties on a large number of Chinese goods imported to the United States. There is a bipartisan consensus in the United States to take a tough stand against

China. The previous American view that engagement with China and helping its peaceful rise will not affect American interests is undergoing a change. There is a growing feeling that America needs to balance its trade relationship with Beijing before China gets too big to compromise. The earlier policy of accommodation is yielding to demonisation of China. And here lies the danger. The tariff war between America and China is turning into a zero-sum game with adverse impacts on the world economy. Some well-considered steps to keep China in check are called for but demonisation of China and getting into a Cold War with it will be a serious mistake. This will hurt both America and China. There are other scholars and academics holding a different point of view. Michael Barkley in an article in *Foreign Affairs* on 21 November, 2018 said that China militarily or strategically will not be able to overtake the United States in the foreseeable future. According to Barkley, China and USA are not caught in a Thucydides trap because China is in no position to challenge the global hegemony of the United States.

16

Sowing the Seeds

The Gaza truce has been a shortlived one. The Israel-Hamas war has resumed in full fury. Meanwhile, America has vetoed the Security Council resolution demanding a ceasefire in Gaza. The US ambassador said that a permanent ceasefire without dismantling Hamas would sow the seeds of a future conflict.

Britain abstained but 13 other members voted in favour of an immediate halt. The US sided with the view of Israel that without eradicating Hamas, lasting peace is not possible. Israel had international sympathy when it launched the campaign to annihilate Hamas, whose fighters stormed across the border on 7 October and killed 1200 Israelis, mostly civilians, and seized 240 hostages. In retaliation, Israel relentlessly bombed Gaza causing death of more than 20,000 Palestinians and injuries to more than 50,000.

Many thousands more are feared lost in rubble or beyond the reach of ambulances. There is an international outcry at this fury of Israel and brutal punishment of the civilians for the terrorist attacks by Hamas. But Israel remains undaunted and determined to carry on the war despite international pressures. Israel's PM Benjamin Netanyahu has declared that Israel will carry on the war until Hamas is annihilated and Israel's decisions will be based on operational considerations. No doubt, dismantling of Hamas is going to be a tough and long drawn out affair and Israel's Defence Minister Yoav Gallant has repeatedly said that Israel will not be swayed by international criticisms and will carry on the war till "its goals are reached". Israel's obduracy is seriously perturbing America.

In fairly blunt criticism, President Biden has criticised the indiscriminate bombing of Gaza by Israel and its lack of interest in the establishment of an independent Palestinian state. America's National Security Adviser, Jake Sullivan visited Gaza to discuss with Israeli leaders a time-table for ending the fighting. He also emphasised the need to make airstrikes by Israel more accurate and not indiscriminate, causing heavy loss of human lives.

It has been estimated that up to 45 per cent of the 29,000 air-to-ground munitions dropped by Israel in Gaza since October 7 have been unguided dumb bombs. Heavy fighting is going on in North Gaza where Hamas fighters are putting up tough resistance. Now Israel's Defence Minister says that fighting may drag on for months and no end is in sight. The Israeli army is also sustaining losses in heavy fighting in Northern Gaza. Israeli officers say that several hundred Israeli soldiers have lost their lives.

On 12 December, the Israeli army suffered one of its highest single day casualties when 10 of its soldiers lost their lives. Soldiers' deaths are a very emotional and sensitive topic in Israel, a small country with compulsory military service. Israeli army leaders estimate that relentless bombing of Gaza and mounting civilian deaths and sufferings will demoralise Hamas and turn the Palestinians away from them.

But that has not happened. Support for Hamas among the bitter and estranged Palestinians has gone up. An opinion poll shows that both in Gaza and in the West Bank, a majority of the Palestinians are supportive of Hamas and disapprove of the Western-backed Dr. Mahmud Abbas of the Palestinian Authority. This shows that the American and Israeli plan of eradication of Hamas as well as creation of a Palestinian state will face heavy weather. There is mounting international criticism of Israel. South

Africa has initiated proceedings against Israel in the International Court of Justice saying that its operations in Gaza amount to genocide, a move that has been welcomed by the Palestinians. Israel has rejected South Africa's move as a "blood libel".

But America is standing by Israel and the Biden administration has approved an emergency weapons sale to Israel bypassing the Congress. There has been an escalation of hostilities in the occupied West Bank as well. Israeli officials have threatened full scale war on Hezbollah if attacks on Israel's North continue. Israel's openly discussed and well-defined plan to ethnically cleanse Gaza and detach it from the Palestinian homeland and to displace the Palestinians in the West Bank will have disastrous repercussions and sow the seeds of a future conflict. As Israel ramps up its operations there is tension with Hezbollah on the Lebanese border and there is the risk of war spilling over. There has been a proposal by Egypt and also by Qatar to resolve the conflict. But neither is moving forward.

The proposals call for release of hostages and a political resolution of the conflict. However, Israel still wants to press ahead with its military goal of crushing Hamas. Indeed, many believe that Gaza cannot be stabilised till Mr. Netanyahu reigns as the Prime Minister. The far-right coalition he heads refuses to do anything to rebuild or expand the Palestinian Authority's role. A credible two-state solution will lead Saudi Arabia as well as other moderate Arab states to normalise relations with Israel and help the cause of peace and security of the region. Of course, it will also bring peace to Israel.

Section 3

17

The Volcano with an Ice Cap

The Central Police Training College (CPTC) at Mount Abu was the training institution for officers selected for the IPS in the 1950s and 1960s. Apart from in-house classes, there were outdoor training courses that were extremely tough.

There was an overwhelming emphasis on drill, parade, physical exercises and horse riding. The underlying premise was that young IPS officers had to be like Spartan Generals—tough, muscular and strong. For the trainees, it was an agonising experience. Those found wanting during the drill and the parade were the butt of acidic comments. Among the outdoor trainers, the most fearsome one was Chief Drill Inspector S. Spadigam. He was an officer of the Malabar Special Police who had been promoted and sent to the CPTC. Short, swarthy and well-built with curly hair and blazing eyes, he was a terror in the parade ground and would roar at us whenever any lapse on our part would come to his notice. He had a repertoire of stinging words and would make lavish use of them without discrimination. While admonishing a trainee for his lacklustre performance in the parade ground, he 'advised' him to die and assured him of a good police funeral. However, despite his rough exterior, he was a well-wisher of young trainee officers and genuinely felt that unless they knew their tradecraft well, they would not be able to command the allegiance of their subordinates. Once, while admonishing some of us, he said IPS officers were the police leaders of tomorrow and they would not be able to lead by example unless they were competent. The dreaded martinet would change completely outside the parade ground. He would be extremely polite and treat us with utmost civility. During our training days, many of us chafed at the undue stress on drill and parade, but now with the wisdom of hindsight, I feel that stamina and physical fitness are direly needed for police work in the field. Spadigam believed that tough training should generate in us a lifelong passion for physical fitness, which unfortunately is missing in many police officers. But he was not just a rough-hewn police officer. He was well-read and well-versed in English literature and would quote lines from Thomas Gray's *Elegy Written in a Country Churchyard* or Coleridge's *The Rime of the Ancient Mariner*. Though quite junior in rank in the police hierarchy, he was never sycophantic and would express his views without equivocation during meetings. The trainees and trainers feared as well as respected him for his total commitment to the job. Generations of IPS officers will never forget this human volcano with an ice cap.

18

The Downfall of a Police Ogre

The National Human Rights Commission (NHRC) created by the Protection of Human Rights Act was passed by the Parliament in 1993. For the first time, in the annals of the country, a Commission was set up exclusively for the protection and promotion of human rights. It is a blue ribbon Commission, with a former Chief Justice of the Supreme Court as the Chairman and includes as members, a Chief Justice of the High Court and a judge of the Supreme Court and an administrator with experience in the field of human rights. I joined as the first Director General in charge of Investigation in the Commission. Since its inception, the Commission was flooded with a large number of complaints of various forms of human rights violations. However, most of the complaints were against the police for violations of human rights.

After I joined Commission, the Chairman asked me to quickly set up an investigation wing in the Commission from the scratch to promptly deal with cases of egregious violation of human rights and place its reports before the Commission, while cautioning that Investigation should be not only non-partisan and above board but must bear the stamp of professional competence. The Ministry of Home Affairs, the nodal ministry, held the view that a skeleton investigation wing would suffice the needs of the

Commission and it could be allowed to utilise the services of the investigation agencies of the Central and State governments. But I felt and explained to the Commission that without an effective investigation wing, it would become a toothless tiger. There were, as expected, serious objections from the government for the sanction of staff proposed by me. But with the decisive intervention of the Commission, the bureaucratic hurdles collapsed like nine pins and our original proposal with minor modifications was accepted and adequate staff was sanctioned.

Very soon, the Commission was deluged with many cases of grotesque violation of human rights and successfully investigated into a number of cases which stirred public attention and received wide coverage in the media. One shocking case of police brutality and insensitivity remains still vivid in my mind. A lady named Rita Dhawan from Ranchi, complained before the Commission that her husband Suresh Dhawan, a businessman and owner of a clothing store in Ranchi, was waylaid and shot dead by the police. The police party led by an inspector, had surrounded his car and demanded one lakh rupees and on his refusal to cough up the amount, shot and killed him. The police on the other hand, had dubbed him as a Naxalite, who had challenged and opened fire at them. At the Commission's instance, a case was registered and the state CID took up the investigation of the case monitored by the NHRC. The case was charge-sheeted but it was hanging fire in the court for a long period.

The Chairman of the Commission in a letter to the Chief Justice of India drew the attention of the latter to the inordinate delay in the disposal of the case. This had the desired quickening effect. The Police Inspector and his cohorts were convicted and sentenced to death. Never before in the past, death penalty was imposed on police personnel for committing an offence like this. The grim outcome pleased me because this would send an appropriate deterrent message to the criminals in uniform. Later, the Apex Court commuted the death sentence to life imprisonment.

The Commission also ordered payment of compensation to the tune of ten lakh to the family of the deceased. However, the State government took the stand that since the accused persons have been convicted and sentenced to death there was no justification in paying compensation, which would impose a financial burden on the state. The Commission disagreed with this contention and pointed out that the culpability of the public servants in a criminal trial and their conviction do not put at rest the claim for compensation for immediate relief to the victims as envisaged under the Protection of Human Rights Act. The culpability of the involved public servants cannot absolve the state of its liability to pay compensation to the victim. The state government complied with the recommendation.

The case also unveiled the shady and seamy past of Inspector Dudh Nath Ram, the villain of the piece. He was earlier a member of a dacoit gang and had cases of dacoity and murder against him. He was also close to Ramsunder Das, who later became the Chief Minister of Bihar for a short period. Utilising his proximity to the Chief Minister, he got a sub-inspector's job in the police without proper verification of his antecedents. He remained corrupt and untrammelled because of his political connections. But due to NHRC's decisive intervention, at last, he got his due desert. The wheels of justice grind slowly but exceedingly fine.

19

Acknowledging Help

A Healing Touch

Rudyard Kipling aptly said that people remember God and police only in distress and never before. When the distress ends, God is forgotten and the police are slighted. However, this observation is not always true. In my long police career, I have witnessed many shining instances of police personnel going out of their way to help those in distress and being gratefully acknowledged for it.

My mind travels back to a case when I was posted as DIG of the Criminal Investigation Department (CID) in Odisha. The department has a squad to trace missing persons. One day, an engineer from the Rourkela steel plant came to meet me. He looked extremely worried. His 12-year-old son had left the house about a week back after a tiff with his mother and the parents had failed to locate him. His wife was distraught and had stopped eating. He himself was passing through unbearable stress and strain.

I told him that the usual practice was to publish a photograph of the boy in newspapers and show slides on television channels. However, it would be better and perhaps more fruitful if he and his wife could visit the probable places his truant son might have gone to.

I deputed a CID Inspector to accompany them so that police help could be sought whenever they visited other states. The father took two weeks' leave and set out with the Inspector. They visited various places in search of the missing boy.

It was a challenging and exhausting endeavour, but the father was optimistic and the Inspector kept on motivating him all through. The police forces in different states rendered full assistance whenever it was sought.

At long last, the patient but agonising search yielded results. With the help of Maharashtra police, the boy was traced to a place near Pune where he was working in a *dhaba*. After the tiff, he along with a friend had landed in Pune.

Tracing the boy brought immense joy and relief to the traumatised parents. I also experienced a rare sense of peace and satisfaction. The CID Inspector felt happy and victorious. He had been a pillar of support.

When the engineer, with tears in his eyes, came to thank me, I told him that I too felt suffused with joy. However, I had a request to make. I wanted him to write letters to newspapers and the electronic media highlighting the help and healing touch he received from the police. Sadly, police failures are trumpeted and good deeds go unheralded.

I felt here was an opportunity to set the record straight, not for my sake, but for the entire police force.

The relieved father kept his word. I also experienced a sense of fulfilment.

20

Human Depravity and Divine Justice

Working in the police department can be satisfying as well as disconcerting. One witnesses cops displaying courage and honesty, while some others commit acts of depravity. I remember a case of police brutality. It was investigated by the Crime Investigation Department (CID) of the Odisha Police. I was then posted as the DIG, CID.

The incident took place at Mundaguda village in Koraput district. Saheb Rath, a bright student of the local high school, was arrested on the charge of stealing books of another student. His father, Parasuram Rath, was a small farmer.

The arrest followed a tiff between Saheb and a local sub-inspector's son, who were both studying in that school. Though he and his father pleaded innocence, they were called to the police station for an interrogation. After preliminary questioning, the officer in charge let the father go but detained the son. The boy dared to ask the cop why he was being victimised.

The officer could not bear this affront. He started hitting the boy with a stick and then kicked him in the chest. The boy did not survive the torture. The scared officer went all out to conceal his crime. With the help of constables and Gram Rakhis, the boy's body was taken to a nearby jungle and tied to an electric pole. A fake entry was made in the station diary of the police station that Saheb attempted to escape from custody. The officer went to the spot to hold an inquest, but irate villagers did not allow him to do so. One villager met the district magistrate and pressed for a judicial inquiry into this case of police torture. The subdivisional magistrate (SDM) was entrusted with the probe. Instead, he came to the rescue of the culprit.

In his inquiry report, the SDM stated that it was a case of suicide, not murder. But following an outrage in the media, the Crime Branch took over the investigation. Its probe revealed a number of ante-mortem injuries; there were swellings and abrasions on the body, caused by kicks and blows.

After the completion of the investigation, the cop was chargesheeted for murder. The conniving constables and Gram Rakhis were charged under Section 201 of the IPC for causing disappearance of evidence of the murder.

However, the Sessions Judge of Koraput acquitted the officer of murder and held him guilty of voluntarily causing hurt; he was given a lenient punishment of three months' imprisonment. The other accused persons were exonerated of the charge of suppression/ disappearance of evidence.

The state government, on the recommendation of the Crime Branch, filed an appeal against the judgement. We were hopeful that the sessions court's order would be overturned by the high court. Meanwhile, the cop's brother, who was helping him fight the case, met with an accident and died. Soon after, the cop suffered a cardiac arrest and passed away. The wheels of justice moved rapidly, thanks to divine retribution.

21

Falling Short of Expectations

My first impression of Police Inspector S. Mohanty was not very flattering. He was in charge of a police circle in Cuttack district of Odisha, while I was posted there as the Assistant Superintendent of Police. A lanky, ungainly fellow with a weather-beaten face, he was the antithesis of a go-getting police officer. During meetings, the Superintendent of Police often used to tick him off for his inadequate supervision of subordinates.

However, it did not take me long to be impressed by Mohanty's personality and style of work. He did not, unlike many police officers, run down his colleagues or make snide comments about seniors. He invariably carried a typewriter and would type out inspection and supervision notes on the spot. He urged me to follow the practice so that the notes were promptly received by subordinates. Despatching notes after returning to the headquarters is often delayed because senior officers get involved in other important tasks and memory starts playing tricks. Mohanty, though not a graduate, had a good command over English. His notes were to the point.

Once, I conducted an inspection of a police station in the Sadar Circle in Mohanty's presence. I appreciated the good work and also pointed out the lapses of the officer in charge and his staff. Some local residents arrived there. I was taken aback by their fulsome praise for the cops. Later, I learnt that this was arranged by the police station staff.

Before leaving, I asked the officer in charge to submit the bill regarding the expenditure incurred in connection with my and my stenographer's board and lodging. He was reluctant to do so and said a senior officer's visit was an honour for the staff, adding that I should not embarrass them by insisting on paying a petty amount. Fresh from training in the National Police Academy, I insisted on making the payment.

It was at this juncture that Mohanty intervened, albeit diffidently. He took me aside and told me that whatever sum I would pay would not match the amount spent by the officer during the inspection. He asked me, instead, to focus on the expectations of subordinates from their senior officers.

Mohanty said the seniors were expected to defend their subordinates when they were right and come down on them like a ton of bricks when they indulged in corrupt practices. Often, subordinate officers got disillusioned when their seniors betrayed the trust reposed in them.

Mohanty's words triggered disquiet. Though occupying leadership positions, many of us fail to inspire our subordinates. They salute us and speak to us deferentially but feel in their heart of hearts that we have been pitchforked into the role of leaders without having the professional and moral qualities expected of us and fail to function as just and capable commanders.

22

A Touching Gesture by a Superior

In December 1977, I was posted as the Deputy Inspector General in charge of investigation in the Justice Shah Commission of Enquiry, which was set up by the then Janata Party government to probe the alleged subversion of lawful processes and established conventions and other excesses committed during the Emergency.

The Secretary of the Commission, P.R. Rajgopal, a former Commissioner of Police, Delhi, would brook no nonsense and make no compromise. But at the same time, he was warm and considerate. He was driving us hard to finish the work within one year allotted to the Commission. Both he and Justice Shah were very clear that our investigations should be transparent and aboveboard and must not be soiled by dubious and questionable methods. To a large extent, this was taken care of.

One day, my wife rang me up and said that our younger son had been experiencing abdominal pain since the morning and had got no relief even after taking painkillers. I returned home in the evening and we took him to a nearby hospital. The doctor was not able to diagnose the ailment and only said that the child had to be kept under observation for a few more hours. With this pronouncement, he left the room and did not return.

Our son was writhing in pain. My wife was in tears and I was at my wits' end, petrified by anxiety and not knowing what was to be done. In that moment of despair, I rang up Rajgopal. He was not at his residence. I left a message that on his return he may ring me at the hospital. Within an hour, Rajgopal called up. I told him about my emergency. His response was prompt. He promised to rush to the hospital with a doctor. True to his word, he arrived with a specialist, who examined my son and said it was a case of acute appendicitis, a rare ailment for a child, and suggested an immediate operation.

At Rajgopal's request, the child specialist himself performed the operation. Later, the doctor told me that it had been a close shave. Delay would have made the operation hazardous and endangered the child's life. My son stayed in the hospital for a few days before being discharged. Soon, he was his old self.

Even now, almost four decades later, I recall that evening in the hospital when Rajgopal appeared like a saviour, not a tough boss but a warm-hearted and compassionate leader with deep concern for his subordinates. Such a spontaneous gesture forges unbreakable bonds between the team leader and his men. Indeed, Rajgopal was a wonderful leader and a grand coordinator. When I expressed my gratitude to him, he simply said: "Just do the same to your subordinates when they turn to you for help."

It was a cold wintry night in Delhi in December 1977. I was at that time posted as the Deputy Inspector General in charge of investigation in the Shah Commission of Enquiry set up by the then Janata Government to enquire into the subversion of lawful processes and established conventions and various other excesses committed during the period of emergency proclaimed by Smt. Indira Gandhi.

Selected complaints were dealt with by the Commission through its own investigative agency. The Commission also took up for open hearing some cases in which there had been blatant abuse of authority and misuse of power and the excesses committed were of gravest magnitude.

Justice Shah was a no-nonsense judge of robust integrity. Fair complexioned, tall and taciturn, Shah was an epitome of judicial propriety and conducted himself with sublime dignity. The Secretary of the Commission, P.R. Rajgopal, former Commissioner of Police, Delhi, was a well-known and reputed officer, who commanded respect and wholesome awe of the subordinates. He was a martinet, who would brook no nonsense and make no compromise in spheres of work and discipline, but at the same time, he was warm and considerate. He also was a hustler driving us hard to accomplish the mission within one year time span of the Commission. Both he and Justice Shah were at the same time very clear that our investigation work should be transparent and above board and must not be soiled by dubious and questionable methods. To a large extent, this could be realized. Though political controversies dogged the steps of the Commission, there had not been any criticisms against the nature and style of functioning of the investigating wing.

The work in the Commission was both challenging as well as exhausting. Voluminous papers and complaints had to be pored over. Many witnesses had to be questioned and veracity of their submissions checked up.

23

A Curious Case of Mistaken Identity

A Commission of Enquiry headed by Justice J.C. Shah was set up by the Janata government after the turbulent period of Emergency, declared by the then Prime Minister Indira Gandhi, to enquire into excesses perpetrated by the previous government during this period.

At that time, I was working as the Assistant Director in the Intelligence Bureau in Jamshedpur. On promotion as DIG, I joined the Enquiry Commission and given the responsibility of investigating into some serious cases of gross abuse of police authority and wanton harassment of the leaders belonging to the opposition parties.

The Commission examined the circumstances leading to the proclamation of emergency and exposed the hollowness of the government claim that emergency was proclaimed because of dire threats to the nation. For investigating into numerous cases filed before the Commission, I along with some officers, who were working with me, had to visit different districts of Haryana.

Bansilal, the then Chief Minister of Haryana, was the prime target of many serious complaints. The investigation work was dry, arduous and painstaking. Justice Shah, however, was determined to complete the work of the Commission within the allotted period of one year.

But it had also some comic interludes. While camping at Hisar, I wanted to visit the new and well-renowned Agricultural University of Hisar and informed the District authorities of my plan accordingly. My limited intention was to get a bird's eye view of the university and its sprawling campus. But by a strange quirk of fate, I was gobsmacked by some unexpected unanticipated events. Mine was an unscheduled private visit and I wanted it to be a simple low-key affair. But to my utter bewilderment, I found that the Vice Chancellor of the University was waiting for me at the portico of the administrative building. He was extremely deferential and was waiting to take me around the sprawling university complex. For the next two hours, the situation turned out to be really Gilbertian. Before l could say anything, the Vice Chancellor started 'sirring' me profusely and explained with great enthusiasm the various/ landmark achievements of the University. An obliging cameraman appeared from nowhere and started clicking the camera.

Accompanied by the Vice Chancellor, I visited the different faculties of the University and the heads of the departments vied with one another to explain to me in all earnestness the latest researches that were being carried out in different departments of the University. I made some amiable, though perhaps not exactly appropriate, remarks.

While I was taken around the library building, the librarian asked me to record my name in the visitor's register. After I had written my name, I could notice a distinct change in the Vice Chancellor's manner. He became a little stiff and standoffish and after a while abruptly took leave of me.

I could sense that something had gone wrong somewhere. The red-carpet welcome and its abrupt end remained to me a riddle wrapped in mystery. I got the answer when my batchmate DIG Hisar told me that someone not kindly disposed towards the Vice

Chancellor, with a puckish sense of humour, had sent a message to him that Justice Shah, Chairman of the Commission would be visiting the University. It was a classic case of mistaken identity.

24

Femme Fatale

During my long years in police profession, I had occasions to investigate and supervise many difficult and sensational crimes, showing human depravity at the lowest. Greed, lust, vengeance, wounded vanity, psychological maladjustments are some of the important causative factors behind commission of these gruesome crimes. But there are instances where a weak and feckless man, under the malevolent influence of a strong-willed vengeful woman is prompted to commit crimes against his better judgement. There are Lady Macbeths in real life.

I have had at the occasion to supervise such a case, I was then posted as the D.I.G. in the Criminal Investigation Department of Odisha Police . The hideous event took place in Dhenkanal district in Odisha. The local police received a report of the brutal murder of the wife of a young engineer, serving in an engineering corporation and her two hapless children, several injuries with a sharp cutting weapon were inflicted on the body of the young lady and the throats of her two little children were slit.

Due to the brutal and sensational nature of the crime and the public outcry that followed, the investigation of the case had to be taken up by the Crime Branch of the Odisha Police. Normally, in State Police Organizations knotty and sensational cases are handed over to the State CID for thorough investigation. During investigation of the case, the CID officers found that the peon of the engineer Padmacharan Behera and his wife Parvati staying in the outhouse of the quarters of the Assistant Engineer S. Subramaniam were missing. Padmacharan was functioning as an office peon and an errand boy while Parvati was a maid servant who cooked food and performed other domestic chores. When I met and interviewed Subramaniam, I found that he was stupefied by the grim tragedy and was totally numbed and dazed. Silent and disobedient tears rolled down his cheeks. Suspicion naturally fell on the fugitives Padmacharan and his wife Parvati for commission of the murder and theft of golden ornaments and other articles from the house. Search for the fugitives began in right earnest. Officers of the crime branch rushed to the native place of the peon Padmacharan in Phulbani district in Odisha and could learn that Padmacharan and Parvati had not come there. Investigation officers could also learn that Padmacharan had a first wife. The determined and indefatigable officers of the Crime Branch without any further loss of time dashed for Parvati's native place in Midnapore district in West Bengal. There they were able to apprehend Padmacharan and Parvati. The couple were completely taken aback as they could never imagine that the Crime Branch officers would dog the trail and apprehend them in their lair at Midnapore. During interrogation, Padmacharan made a clean-breast confession of the crime. He said that while serving in Subramaniam's house as a peon, he came to know Parvati, the Bengali maid working there. Parvati was good-looking and physically attractive. Padmacharan soon came completely under the bewitching spell of Parvati and turned to a puppet under her total control. Parvati was strong-willed and temperamental and was not getting along well with Subramaniam's wife Jenova, who used to often scold her for shoddy and perfunctory works. When Subramaniam went alone to attend a family function at Tamil Nadu, Parvati and Padmacharan felt this was the right time to carry out their macabre scheme. On the night of 24th July, Parvati slept in the house along with Jenova and the two children.

As per prearranged plan, Parvati at the dead of night opened the door from inside. Padmacharan tiptoed in with a long sharp knife, which he had borrowed from a neighbour for slicing vegetables. Together, they strangled Jenova to death and then slit the throats of the children. Parvati then removed the golden nose flowers and ear-rings from the dead body of Jenova and after ransacking the bedroom decamped with other valuables.

During interrogation by the police, Parvati candidly said that she had decided to start a new life with Padmacharan, because her first husband ill-treated her. However, she did not know that Padmacharan was already married as he kept it a secret. She said that daily rebukes and insults heaped on her by Jenova had become unbearable and she wanted to settle scores with her. However, it was not their intention to kill the innocent children but had no other alternative, when they raised an alarm. Both said that by no stretch of imagination they could think that the police from Odisha would dog their trail and catch them at Midnapore in Bengal.

After a thorough investigation, the Crime Branch officers submitted the charge-sheet. During the test identification parade, Subramaniam identified the stolen items. Blood stains on the seized knife contained blood group B, which matched with that of Jenova and one son. During trial, the defence took the plea that Subramaniam was present in the house, on that fateful night and it was he who had murdered Jenova and his sons because of his lust for untainted Parvati. This untenable plea was rejected by the court and the Sessions Judge convicted the accused under Section 302 IPC and sentenced them to rigorous imprisonment for life. The Bard of Avon had aptly said that "hell knoweth no fury than a woman scorned." Life of a young Engineer was shattered and ruined by love and lust of a vengeful woman and her, weakling, wimpish accomplice I do not know if young Subramaiam was able to overcome the shattering blow and move on with this devastating tragedy.

25

Suicide Bombing

It is reported in the press that in Pakistan, 12 security personnel were killed last month when a suicide bomber rammed an explosive-laden vehicle into a check-post in Pakistan's north-western Khyber Pakhtunkhwa province. Of late, there has been an escalation of suicide bombing attacks by terrorists in Pakistan. Hafis Gul Bahadur, a militant organisation affiliated with the Tehriki-Taliban Pakistan, claimed responsibility for this night raid. Pakistan says that TTP, which the USA lists as a global terrorist organisation, is orchestrating the deadly violence from sanctuaries in Afghanistan.

Kabul has stoutly denied the allegations. Suicide bombing is becoming the most dreaded form of terrorist attack in many countries of the world. In India, suicide bombing was not witnessed in the early days of terrorism in Kashmir and Punjab. The first and most daring case of suicide bombing was the assassination of Rajiv Gandhi by LTTE cadres in 1991. The Chief Minister of Punjab, Sardar Beant Singh was the next victim of suicide terrorism in Chandigarh in August 1995. The first suicide bombing in Kashmir took place in April 1999, in the Badami Bagh area of Srinagar, when a Jaish militant launched a suicide attack on Indian Army 15 Corps Headquarters.

Suicide bombing first hogged the limelight in April 1983, when the terrorist network of Hezbollah attacked the American Embassy in Beirut, and later, in the same year, devastated the US Marine Headquarters in Lebanon. The success of the Hezbollah suicide bombing inspired the Liberation Tigers of Tamil Eelam to resort to suicide bombings on a huge scale in their operations. The suicide bombers constituted an elite corps and occupied a privileged position in LTTE. They were separated from ordinary cadre, and kept in isolation. The Tigers are perhaps the only terrorist outfit responsible for the assassination of two former prime ministers—Rajiv Gandhi and Premadasa of Sri Lanka. LTTE's suicide missions were planned with minute attention to detail, and precisely executed with lethal impact.

The LTTE cadre responsible for the assassination of Premadasa infiltrated into his staff, and remained inactive for nearly two years, before embarking on the deadly mission. Research in the field has shown that most suicide bombing missions are not "lone wolf" operations. They are meticulously planned by a terrorist network. The suicide bombers are trained, motivated and radicalised before being sent on their missions. For organizing successful bombing operations, there is need for extensive underground preparation and coordination. Explosives have to be smuggled and stored properly and safely, for which reliable local support is needed.

The damage inflicted by suicide bombings is both physical and psychological, and to inflict maximum damage the bombers rely heavily on the element of surprise. Surprise is generated by turning the everyday into a weapon. For instance, suicide bombers often wear their explosives underneath their clothing, carry them in backpacks, or even hide them in bicycle frames. Frequently, to inflict even greater damage, suicide bombers drive vehicles packed with explosives into the targets. The use of suicide bombing has grown for three main reasons. First, suicide bombing is almost impossible for security forces to prevent. Second, media attention is almost like oxygen to the terrorist and suicide bombings generate great publicity and receive enormous news coverage. Third, suicide bombings require little expertise and few resources beyond a bomb and someone willing to carry it, thus is more cost effective than other tactics.

The growth in suicide bombing has often been linked to the rise of religion-inspired terrorist violence, but this is not totally correct. American political scientist Robert Pape has argued that prior to 2003, a group that often resorted to suicide bombings was LTTE, a secular, separatist, ethnic group from Sri Lanka. Though religion is often misused to justify suicide bombings, studies have shown that many suicide bombers, particularly in developed societies, are not fanatics and a significant number of bombers come from income and education levels well above their country's norms. Suicide bombers pose serious security hazards. It is very difficult to detect and prevent such bombers, who can always spring a surprise.

But, the task of suicide bombers can be made more difficult and burdensome, and the impact of the strike may be reduced by adopting various measures like strict access control, strengthening of verification procedures etc. There should be constant training and drill of the security personnel deployed for protection of VIPs and other possible targets and sensitive installations. There are instances where alertness of the security staff has prevented, or foiled lethal strikes. Regular briefing and constant simulated exercises are necessary to hone skills, and sharpen responses. Along with the refinement of skills, there should be upgradation of equipment and weaponry available to the security personnel.

Index